OPPOSING
VIEWPOINTS®
SERIES

Media Violence

Other Books of Related Interest:

Opposing Viewpoints Series

Popular Culture

At Issue Series

Policing the Internet

Current Controversies Series

Media Ethics

> "Congress shall make no law ... abridging the freedom of speech, or of the press."
>
> *First Amendment to the US Constitution*

The basic foundation of our democracy is the First Amendment guarantee of freedom of expression. The Opposing Viewpoints Series is dedicated to the concept of this basic freedom and the idea that it is more important to practice it than to enshrine it.

**OPPOSING
VIEWPOINTS®
SERIES**

Media Violence

Noah Berlatsky, Book Editor

GREENHAVEN PRESS
A part of Gale, Cengage Learning

GALE
CENGAGE Learning·

Detroit • New York • San Francisco • New Haven, Conn • Waterville, Maine • London

Elizabeth Des Chenes, *Director, Publishing Solutions*

© 2012 Greenhaven Press, a part of Gale, Cengage Learning

Gale and Greenhaven Press are registered trademarks used herein under license.

For more information, contact:
Greenhaven Press
27500 Drake Rd.
Farmington Hills, MI 48331-3535
Or you can visit our Internet site at gale.cengage.com.

For product information and technology assistance, contact us at:

Gale Customer Support, 1-800-877-4253.
For permission to use material from this text or product, submit all requests online at www.cengage.com/permissions.

Further permissions questions can be emailed to permissionrequest@cengage.com.

Articles in Greenhaven Press anthologies are often edited for length to meet page requirements. In addition, original titles of these works are changed to clearly present the main thesis and to explicitly indicate the author's opinion. Every effort is made to ensure that Greenhaven Press accurately reflects the original intent of the authors. Every effort has been made to trace the owners of copyrighted material.

Cover image © DonSmith/Alamy

LIBRARY OF CONGRESS CATALOGING-IN-PUBLICATION DATA

Media violence / Noah Berlatsky, book editor.
     p. cm. -- (Opposing viewpoints)
     Includes bibliographical references and index.
     ISBN 978-0-7377-6328-7 (hardcover) -- ISBN 978-0-7377-6329-4 (pbk.)
    1. Violence in mass media--Juvenile literature. 2. Mass media and children--Juvenile literature. I. Berlatsky, Noah.
     P96.V5M425 2012
     303.6--dc23

                            2012005719

Printed in the United States of America
1 2 3 4 5 6 7 16 15 14 13 12

Contents

Chapter 3: What Is the Effect of Violence in the News?

Chapter 4: What Is the Relationship Between Violence and Sex in the Media?

Why Consider Opposing Viewpoints?

> *"The only way in which a human being can make some approach to knowing the whole of a subject is by hearing what can be said about it by persons of every variety of opinion and studying all modes in which it can be looked at by every character of mind. No wise man ever acquired his wisdom in any mode but this."*
>
> *John Stuart Mill*

In our media-intensive culture it is not difficult to find differing opinions. Thousands of newspapers and magazines and dozens of radio and television talk shows resound with differing points of view. The difficulty lies in deciding which opinion to agree with and which "experts" seem the most credible. The more inundated we become with differing opinions and claims, the more essential it is to hone critical reading and thinking skills to evaluate these ideas. Opposing Viewpoints books address this problem directly by presenting stimulating debates that can be used to enhance and teach these skills. The varied opinions contained in each book examine many different aspects of a single issue. While examining these conveniently edited opposing views, readers can develop critical thinking skills such as the ability to compare and contrast authors' credibility, facts, argumentation styles, use of persuasive techniques, and other stylistic tools. In short, the Opposing Viewpoints Series is an ideal way to attain the higher-level thinking and reading skills so essential in a culture of diverse and contradictory opinions.

In addition to providing a tool for critical thinking, Opposing Viewpoints books challenge readers to question their own strongly held opinions and assumptions. Most people form their opinions on the basis of upbringing, peer pressure, and personal, cultural, or professional bias. By reading carefully balanced opposing views, readers must directly confront new ideas as well as the opinions of those with whom they disagree. This is not to argue simplistically that everyone who reads opposing views will—or should—change his or her opinion. Instead, the series enhances readers' understanding of their own views by encouraging confrontation with opposing ideas. Careful examination of others' views can lead to the readers' understanding of the logical inconsistencies in their own opinions, perspective on why they hold an opinion, and the consideration of the possibility that their opinion requires further evaluation.

Evaluating Other Opinions

To ensure that this type of examination occurs, Opposing Viewpoints books present all types of opinions. Prominent spokespeople on different sides of each issue as well as well-known professionals from many disciplines challenge the reader. An additional goal of the series is to provide a forum for other, less known, or even unpopular viewpoints. The opinion of an ordinary person who has had to make the decision to cut off life support from a terminally ill relative, for example, may be just as valuable and provide just as much insight as a medical ethicist's professional opinion. The editors have two additional purposes in including these less known views. One, the editors encourage readers to respect others' opinions—even when not enhanced by professional credibility. It is only by reading or listening to and objectively evaluating others' ideas that one can determine whether they are worthy of consideration. Two, the inclusion of such viewpoints encourages the important critical thinking skill of objectively evaluating an author's credentials and bias. This evaluation will illuminate an author's reasons for taking a particular stance on an issue and will aid in readers' evaluation of the author's ideas.

It is our hope that these books will give readers a deeper understanding of the issues debated and an appreciation of the complexity of even seemingly simple issues when good and honest people disagree. This awareness is particularly important in a democratic society such as ours in which people enter into public debate to determine the common good. Those with whom one disagrees should not be regarded as enemies but rather as people whose views deserve careful examination and may shed light on one's own.

Thomas Jefferson once said that "difference of opinion leads to inquiry, and inquiry to truth." Jefferson, a broadly educated man, argued that "if a nation expects to be ignorant and free . . . it expects what never was and never will be." As individuals and as a nation, it is imperative that we consider the opinions of others and examine them with skill and discernment. The Opposing Viewpoints Series is intended to help readers achieve this goal.

David L. Bender and Bruno Leone,
Founders

Introduction

Horror films show graphic death scenes with bodies missing limbs and spurting blood. Rap music and video games feature shootings and beatings. Even young adult novels such as Suzanne Collins's *The Hunger Games* include scenes with children murdering each other. There's no doubt that violent media are popular. The question is why?

Some have argued that humans have a biological desire for violence, just as they have a biological desire for sex. Jeanne Bryner, in a January 17, 2008, article in *LiveScience*, reports on research in which mice seemed to seek out fights just for the sake of the fight itself. Study team member Craig Kennedy, a professor of special education and pediatrics at Vanderbilt University, notes that "Aggression occurs among virtually all vertebrates and is necessary to get and keep important resources such as mates, territory and food." He says the study showed that for mice a "reward pathway in the brain" is involved in aggressive behavior. Aggression, therefore, becomes its own reward. From this perspective, consuming violent media could be seen as fulfilling a biological imperative for humans.

Others argue that humans consume violent media for social rather than biological reasons. In her book *Shocking Entertainment: Viewer Response to Violent Movies*, Annette Hill points out that people often watch violent movies with others and enjoy comparing reactions. People know that violent movies are supposed to test boundaries and enjoy seeing how much they can stand.

Hill also notes that real violence and violent entertainment are very different. She says,

> Active consumers of violent movies do not find real violence in any way entertaining, and they differentiate between real violence and fictional violence. In many ways, it is because they abhor real violence that those viewers I spoke to chose to watch fictional violence . . . it is a safe way of understanding response to violence without having to experience violence in real life.

Rather than for biological or social reasons, appreciation of media violence may be aesthetic. That is, people may find beauty in representations of violence. Charles Reece holds this view in a March 23, 2008, post on *Amoeblog* discussing Michael Haneke's 2007 film *Funny Games*. Reece maintains that violence has been "as much—if not more—a determining factor in the creation of what now constitutes [the] civilized self than our love for beautiful things." His favorite scene in the film is one in which a couple has just had its child murdered. The two, George and Anna, are tied up in their living room; Anna struggles to her feet to turn off the television set so she can weep in quiet. Reece says, "It's a morbidly beautiful scene, and I don't feel the least bit guilty for seeing it as such."

All of these explanations suggest that interest in violence is to some extent normal or natural. Some have argued, though, that the enthusiasm for violent media is part of a social problem. In

1999's *Tough Guise: Violence, Media and the Crisis of Masculinity*, documentary filmmaker Jackson Katz asserts that violence and aggression are part of what society expects from young men. He maintains that outbreaks of violence and enthusiasm for violent media are signs of the misguided way in which we think about masculinity. Sam Hine, a writer for *Catholicplanet.com*, claims that real-life shootings and "the glorification of violence and sexual predation in films," as well as violent video games and other media violence, are all part of a "violent and sick culture." For Katz and Hine, the answer to why we like violence is that we and our society are broken.

While Katz and Hine believe media violence reflects societal ills, others don't believe the consumption of violent media is a problem at all. *Opposing Viewpoints: Media Violence* addresses the controversies surrounding violent media in the following chapters: Is Media Violence a Serious Problem? How Should Media Violence Be Regulated? What Is the Effect of Violence in the News? and What Is the Relationship Between Violence and Sex in the Media?

OPPOSING
VIEWPOINTS®
SERIES

CHAPTER 1

Is Media Violence a Serious Problem?

Chapter Preface

One of the most contentious issues in US politics is the debate over gun policy. Advocates of greater gun control argue that the ready availability of handguns contributes to the United States' high murder rate. "The highest homicide rate of any affluent democracy, nearly four times that of France and the United Kingdom, and six times that of Germany," writes Jill Lepore in a November 9, 2009, article in the *New Yorker*. But those opposed to gun regulation argue that freedom to own handguns is guaranteed by the Second Amendment to the US Constitution. "Handguns are used for protection more often than they are used to commit violent crimes," states an article on the National Rifle Association's website.

The debate about handgun regulation is mirrored by the debate about handguns in the media. Many people argue that the use of guns in movies, music videos, and rap lyrics has glamorized violence. For instance, the Glock pistol has become a popular weapon in part because of its high media profile. As Andrew Martin writes in a January 14, 2011, *New York Times* article, Glocks "are easy to conceal, powerful and hold more ammunition than the old revolvers." They have been used in numerous tragic shootings, including the January 2011 shooting that killed six people in Arizona and wounded US Representative Gabrielle Giffords as well as the 2007 shooting at Virginia Tech that left thirty-two dead.

Anti-gun campaigners maintain that the use of guns in video games can be particularly dangerous, because the games teach players to shoot guns at live targets. In a 2000 interview in *Executive Intelligence Review*, David Grossman said that the game Time Crisis was a "*murder* simulator. . . . It is a device placed in the hands of children, whose only social characteristic is to give him the skill and the will to kill."

Gun advocates, on the other hand, argue that the media portray guns and gun owners in a negative light. In a September 30,

2011, Fox News article, John Lott contends that after the Supreme Court declared that gun bans in Chicago and Washington, DC, were unconstitutional, murder and crime rates in both cities fell. Although this suggests that making guns more available fosters safer cities, Lott asserts that "the national media have been completely silent about this news."

In the middle of the spectrum are those who are not pro- or anti-gun but do not believe that guns in the media harm society. In an article for the Media Awareness Network, psychiatrist Serge Tisseron writes, "Just because a film has a murder scene doesn't mean people are going to commit the act."

The viewpoints in the following chapter further examine controversies surrounding whether media violence is a serious problem.

> *"All of this media access does have an*
> *influence on a variety of health issues."*

Media Violence Causes Aggression

NewsRx Health and Science

NewsRx is a media company and one of the world's largest publishers of health news. In the following viewpoint, the authors argue that media violence and sexual content influence young minds. Children spend many hours a day with media, making it difficult for parents to monitor their children's media habits. The viewpoint claims that children learn their attitudes toward violence at a young age and that makes it difficult to reverse and modify these attitudes.

As you read, consider the following questions:

1. According to the article, how many hours a day do children spend with media?
2. As stated in the viewpoint, what percentage of real-life violence is attributed to media violence?
3. What are some ways parents can change the way their children access media?

With children having easier access to media and a wider variety of content, the possible negative influence on health issues such as sex, drugs, obesity and eating disorders is increased, and warrants monitoring usage and limiting access if necessary, according to a commentary in the June 3 [2009] issue of JAMA [Journal of the American Medical Association], a theme issue on child and adolescent health.

Victor C. Strasburger, M.D., of the University of New Mexico School of Medicine, Albuquerque, presented the commentary at a JAMA media briefing in New York.

On average, children and adolescents spend more than 6 hours a day with media—more time than in formal classroom instruction, writes Dr. Strasburger. In addition, U.S. youth have unprecedented access to media (two-thirds have a television set in their bedrooms, half have a VCR or DVD player, half have a video game console, and almost one-third have Internet access or a computer), making parental monitoring of media use difficult.

All of this media access does have an influence on a variety of health issues, according to Dr. Strasburger. "The media are not the leading cause of any pediatric health problem in the United States, but they do make a substantial contribution to many health problems, including the following."

Media Violence, Sex, and Drugs

Violence. Research on media violence and its relationship to real-life aggression is substantial and convincing. Young persons learn their attitudes about violence at a very young age and, once learned, those attitudes are difficult to modify. Conservative estimates are that media violence may be associated with 10 percent of real-life violence.

Sex. Several longitudinal studies have linked exposure to sex in the media to earlier onset of sexual intercourse. The media represent an important access point for birth control information for youth; however, the major networks continue to balk at airing

The Scientific Debate on Media Violence Is Over

The scientific debate about whether exposure to media violence causes increases in aggressive behavior is over and should have been over 30 years ago. The entire body of relevant media violence research stretches back over 50 years and includes studies on violent television, films, video games, music, and even comic books. Populations studied include males and females; young children, adolescents, and adults; criminals and non-criminals; highly aggressive and nonaggressive people. All major types of research methodologies have been used. . . .

A panel of leading media violence researchers organized by Professor Rowell Huesmann . . . conducted the most comprehensive review to date of media violence effects on aggression and aggression-related variables. This panel found "unequivocal evidence that media violence increases the likelihood of aggressive and violent behavior in both immediate and long-term contexts."

Craig Alan Anderson, Douglas A. Gentile, and Katherine E. Buckley, Violent Video Game Effects on Children and Adolescents: Theory, Research and Public Policy. *New York: Oxford University Press, 2007, p. 4.*

contraception advertisements at the same time they are airing unprecedented amounts of sexual situations and innuendoes in their primetime programs.

Drugs. Witnessing smoking scenes in movies may be the leading factor associated with smoking initiation among youth. In addition, young persons can be heavily influenced by alcohol and cigarette advertising. More than $20 billion a year is spent in the United States on advertising cigarettes ($13 billion), alcohol ($5 billion), and prescription drugs ($4 billion).

Obesity and Eating Disorders

Obesity. Media use is implicated in the current epidemic of obesity worldwide, but it is unclear how. Children and adolescents view an estimated 7,500 food advertisements per year, most of which are for junk food or fast food. Contributing factors to obesity may include that watching television changes eating habits and media use displaces more active physical pursuits.

Eating Disorders. The media are a major contributor to the formation of an adolescent's body self-image. In Fiji, a naturalistic study of teenage girls found that the prevalence of eating disorders increased dramatically after the introduction of American TV programs.

Dr. Strasburger adds that network contraceptive advertising should be encouraged and legislation should be passed banning all cigarette advertising in all media and limiting alcohol advertising to advertisements that only show the product.

Education of parents, teachers, and clinicians about these issues is necessary, and education of students about the media should be mandatory in schools. "Parents have to change the way their children access the media—not permitting TV sets or Internet connections in the child's bedroom, limiting entertainment screen time to less than 2 hours per day, and co-viewing with their children and adolescents. Research has shown that media effects are magnified significantly when there is a TV set in the child's or adolescent's bedroom."

*"In the aggregate the research
says that media violence
does not correlate
to aggression."*

Watching Doesn't Make Us Violent: Assessing the Research on Media Violence

David Trend

In the following viewpoint, University of California professor David Trend contends that most scientific studies of the effects of media violence have been inconclusive. He says that studies are generally flawed in their methods, in part because studying the relationship between people and entertainment is very complicated. The results that have been produced, he argues, show little correlation between viewing media and increased aggression. For political reasons, however, he says, links between media and aggression are often exaggerated. Trend is a professor of studio art at the University of California, Irvine.

As you read, consider the following questions:

1. What does Trend say are two big problems of scientifically studying the effects of media violence?
2. Why are laboratory experiments the largest category of research on media violence, according to Trend?
3. What problems did Richard Rhodes find with the study of media violence by Eron and Huesmann?

What about children? It is commonly assumed that children are more attracted to violent imagery and more vulnerable to its harmful effects, especially when it comes to imitation. Bruno Bettelheim is largely responsible for a belief circulated in the 1970s that children had a "natural" attraction to violence. In his widely read *The Uses of Enchantment: The Meaning and Importance of Fairy Tales*,[1] Bettelheim asserted that frightening stories help kids to understand their innate aggressive tendencies and to eventually control them as adults. These beliefs persist today and provide rationalizations, not only for the continued exposure that children experience through traditional fairy tales like "Little Red Riding Hood" and "Hansel and Gretel," but also in the invariably violent narratives of Disney feature films like *Chronicles of Narnia* (2005) and *Pirates of the Caribbean: Dead Man's Chest* (2006) that feature violent death as primary plot ingredients. Writing of the widespread use of violence in children's media, Maria Tatar states that "Bettelheim's views [becoming] the prevailing orthodoxy on fairy tales is symptomatic of our cultural willingness to embrace the view that 'delinquent and violent' tendencies are part of human nature and that children, in particular, must learn to manage this innate behavior."[2]

---

1. Bruno Bettelheim, *The Uses of Enchantment: The Meaning and Importance of Fairy Tales* (New York: Knopf, 1976).
2. Maria Tatar, "'Violent Delights' in Children's Literature," in Goldstein, *Why We Watch*, p. 71.

Children and Violence

Yet nowhere in the literature or science of media violence has there been any documentation that children are naturally disposed to violence. Despite this paucity of evidence, children remain at the center of the media violence debate. In part this is because topics like "childhood," "children's welfare," and "the death of childhood" work so effectively in emotionalizing political arguments. The meanings of such terms can be quite variable, ranging from references to innocent children that need adult protection, to menacing children who take weapons to school, to the inner child, the childlike adult, and the adult-like child. In other words, childhood is not a natural or fixed category. It is a screen upon which adults project their social anxieties and desires. The figure of the child has been used historically to promote issues ranging from environmentalism ("children inherit the earth") to tax reform ("mortgaging our children's future"). David Buckingham writes about the "politics of substitution" that childhood enables:

> In a climate of growing uncertainty, invoking fears about children provides a powerful means of commanding public attention and support: campaigns against homosexuality are redefined as campaigns against pedophiles; campaigns against pornography become campaigns against child pornography; campaigns against immorality and Satanism become campaigns against ritualistic child abuse. Those who have the temerity to doubt claims about the epidemic proportions of such phenomena can easily therefore be stigmatized as hostile to children.[3]

When all else fails in the media violence debate, proponents of surveillance and censorship haul out the image of the helpless

---

3. David Buckingham, *After the Death of Childhood: Growing Up in the Age of Electronic Media* (Cambridge: Polity, 2000), p. 11.

and vulnerable child. While it is true that children don't have the same capabilities as adults, it can also be said that these projections at times discredit the intelligence of young people and contribute to a distorted infantilization. Close examination of children's responses to violent cartoons, for example, reveals that they more often respond to the excitement or excess of imagery in general, what Tatar terms "burlesque violence," than to the purposeful brutality of "retaliatory violence." When children write their own fairy tales, they tend to avoid this latter type of violence and write happy endings for all of the characters.[4] Like adults, children do revel in the arousal and excitement of aggressive representation in what Michael Zuckerman termed the "sensation seeking" motive.[5] Parents often worry about children over-identifying with perpetrators of television or movie violence. Surprisingly, there is very little data on this. What the research has shown is that most children don't imagine themselves committing violence, although roughly half empathize with victims of violence.[6] Even less plausible is the "forbidden fruit" theory that children's desire is increased if attempts are made to restrict access to a program. A variety of studies in the 1970s disproved this widely accepted theory.[7]

Researching the Effects of Media Violence

Groups seeking to influence public policy know the importance of "objective" research in making their claims. Psychologists and other social scientists have sought to correlate exposure to violent media with certain "effects" among viewers—such as aggression, desensitization, or fear. Often this involves laboratory research studies in which violent films or videos are shown to groups of

4. Ibid., p. 72.
5. Michael Zuckerman, *Sensation Seeking: Beyond the Optimal Level of Arousal* (New York: Wiley, 1979).
6. Maria Tatar, "'Violent Delights,'" p. 98.
7. Ibid., p. 99.

children or adults, who subsequently answer questions about aggression. These findings are compared to those from a control group exposed to non-violent media. Some researchers observe the behavior of study subjects after viewing the media or they create situations where aggressive acts (hitting an inflatable doll, for example) may take place. Frequently in these experiments, viewers of violent media do indeed exhibit relatively small and short-term predilections for increased aggression. Laboratory experiments have led researchers to believe that media violence leads people to imitate what they see on the screen in their own lives. How does this work? According to psychologist Leonard Berkowitz, aggressive behavior occurs when viewers of violent media experience situations that remind them of something they've seen in a representation.[8] Another psychologist, Dolf Zillmann, asserts that violent media make viewers so excited that ordinary behaviors become amplified into violent ones.[9]

Other empirical research employs surveys or data analysis conducted outside the laboratory. The more nuanced of these seek to measure the effect of long-term exposure to media violence, rather than the cause-and-effect consequence of a single viewing. This move into what has been termed "cultivation" research is seen as a more naturalistic approach to the measurement of media effects. One of the originators of cultivation theory, George Gerbner, writes, "Television is a centralized system of storytelling. Its drama, commercials, news, and other programs bring a relatively coherent system of images and messages into every home. That system cultivates from infancy the predisposition and preferences that used to be acquired from other 'primary sources.'"[10] In this light, cultivation describes the

8. Leonard Berkowitz, "Some Effects of Observed Aggression," *Journal of Personality and Social Psychology*, 2 (1965): 359–69.
9. Zillmann, "The Psychology of the Appeal of Portrayals of Violence."
10. George Gerbner, Michael Gross, Michael Morgan, Nancy Signorielli, and James Shanahan, "Growing Up with Television: Cultivation Processes," in Jennings Bryant and Dolf Zillman, eds., *Media Effects: Advances in Theory and Research* (Mahwah, NJ: Lawrence Erlbaum Associates, 2002), p. 47.

"contributions television viewing makes to viewer conceptions of social reality."[11]

Generally speaking, there are two big problems in "scientifically" studying media violence. The first problem stems from how terribly difficult it is to study complex human behavior. A researcher first needs to figure out how to isolate the behavior and then to establish whether one thing or many things cause it. Human violence is influenced by many elements: brain chemistry, environment, upbringing, culture, and the immediate circumstances around it. Studying any one of these factors by itself is quite a challenge. Then add the complexity of the ways people consume, interpret, and are influenced by the media. People do not simply view a TV show or a deodorant advertisement and then robotically go out and act upon this experience. They enjoy, transform, reject, ignore, remember or forget the messages they receive. How do you study that?

The second problem has to do with logic. Most scientific studies set out to prove a correlation between watching violent media and a behavioral change. Perhaps a study shows that boys who see the *Doom* or *King Kong* (both 2005) movies are more likely to smash their toys. There is a correlation between watching the movies and doing the smashing. But this doesn't necessarily mean that the boys responded because of the movie. Perhaps a portion of the movie or an external element affected their behavior. Simple as this sounds, this problem of logic has dogged much of the science on media violence. Well-designed research studies can rule out some of the distorting effects of outside variables, but such studies are expensive and time-consuming. Major categories of empirical media violence research include laboratory research, field studies, and longitudinal (long-term) research.

---

11. Ibid., p. 44.

Laboratory and Field Research

When most people think about the science of media violence they are thinking about laboratory research findings. This is the largest category of research and the one type of research capable of clearly proving cause-and-effect relationships. It is relatively quick and less expensive than extensive studies involving field research, interviews, or the long-term tracking of research subjects. For all of these reasons, empirical findings from laboratory experiments have been sought by groups seeking definitive answers about media violence. Laboratory experiments have been the centerpiece of what has been called the "effects" field in media violence.

Overall, the laboratory studies of the effects of media violence have shown small, short-term increases in aggressive behavior among participants viewing violent material. In one early and widely referenced study conducted in the 1960s by O.I. Lovaas, children in several cohorts were exposed to violent and non-violent cartoons.[12] In one of the cohorts the children who had seen the violent material exhibited a slightly more violent attitude immediately afterwards. In another group, viewers of both violent and non-violent films became more aggressive. Although the study was publicized later as "proving" the negative effects of media violence, the amount of influence the films had was relatively small and not long-acting. In another study conducted by C.W. Mueller and E. Donnerstein, subjects viewed aggressive, humorous, or neutral films and then were offered the chance to act aggressively.[13] Participants who had seen the aggressive or humorous films were more aggressive than those who had seen the neutral material. But in this instance no significant difference could be found between responses to the aggressive and the

12. O. I. Lovaas, "Effects of Exposure to Symbolic Expression on Aggressive Behaviour," *Child Development*, 32 (1961): 37–44.
13. C. W. Mueller and E. Donnerstein, "Film Induced Arousal and Aggressive Behavior," *Journal of Social Psychology*, 119, no. 1 (1983): pp. 61–7.

humorous films, leading observers to conclude that the aggressive behavior might have resulted from being excited or from "arousal," as one paper expressed it. These studies typify much of the laboratory research on media violence in that they can be said to have yielded evidence about the effects of viewing aggressive material. But they have been criticized for the overall weakness of their findings.

One of the most comprehensive assessments of media violence laboratory research was conducted in the late 1990s by psychologist Jonathan L. Freedman.[14] According to Freedman, many references by groups like the American Medical Association and the American Academy of Psychiatry to large numbers of media violence studies—ranging from 1,000 to 3,500 in some accounts—can be sourced to a single frequently cited statement in a National Institute of Mental Health report of the 1980s that there existed approximately 2,500 *publications* on the topic. This is hardly the same as a comparable number of empirical studies. Freedman suggests that the question of the number of studies may really be an issue of semantics. After exhaustive investigation, Freedman found that the media violence "effects" literature actually consisted of 200 pieces of non-duplicated research of varying degrees of scientific legitimacy. The most credible of these studies were able to document but minimal correlations or trace "effects" resulting in increased aggressive behavior among those studied.

Most often the effects of media violence were demonstrated through laboratory experiments, which in more recent years have been criticized for the way they decontextualize media in environments quite unlike everyday viewing. Of the 87 laboratory experiments Freedman examined, he asserts that 37 percent supported the effects hypothesis, 41 percent disproved it, and 22 percent were inconclusive. This means that in the aggregate

14. Freedman, *Media Violence*.

the research says that media violence *does not correlate* to aggression. Studies using survey techniques produced similar ambiguities, showing an aggregate positive correlation between violent media and aggression between 0.1 and 0.2. This means that the studies were able to show that but 1–4 percent of the aggression expressed by the people surveyed could be attributed to media violence. Statisticians would consider this an extremely weak correlation. These findings were compromised further in their use of smaller samples. Also, many failed when attempts were made to reproduce the findings in a second study.[15]

Finally, there are several other problems with laboratory research. The most commonly heard is that the laboratory experimentation takes place in an environment dramatically different from one where the effects of media violence might be diluted by distraction, conversation, or outside influence. Also, laboratory research is more vulnerable to what has been termed "experimenter demand," that is, the thinking by research subjects that they are expected to exhibit some kind of behavior because of the experiment. Put another way, the artificiality of the laboratory environment makes people behave differently than they would normally.

Field experiments constitute another broad category of effects, generally favored because they provide a more natural environment than the laboratory. They also tend to be more long-term. As discussed in the introduction to [*The Myth of Media Violence: A Critical Introduction*], one of the most famous field studies was carried out in 1971 by Feshbach and Singer, who studied 625 boys in seven residential boarding academies and reform schools in California and New York.[16] In both types of institution the boys' access to television was controlled for six weeks, with half being permitted to watch only non-violent programs and the other violent shows. Astonishingly, the boys in the violent

15. All statistics from Freedman, *Media Violence*.
16. Feshbach and Singer, *Television and Aggression*.

program cohort exhibited fewer acts of violent behavior—like acting up in class, fighting, or breaking things—than the non-violent cohort. It turned out that the non-violent cohort were made unhappy because they couldn't watch their favorite violent shows. While many other field experiments have shown a relationship between viewing violence and aggressive behavior, the Feshbach and Singer study holds significance in pointing out one of the major drawbacks of field research. Studying groups in natural environments over long periods of time limits the researchers' ability to correct for extraneous factors that might muddle their findings. In this case researchers didn't take into account the effect of the boys' existing viewing preferences—and that those preferences might override or cause a backfire in how the boys reacted to the study protocol.

Long-Term Research

The most famous study of the long-term effects of media violence was conducted from 1960 to 1982 by psychologists Leonard D. Eron and L. Rowell Huesmann.[17] The idea behind what came to be called the "22-Year Study" was to look at the difference between children who grew up with violent media and those who were not exposed to such material. Over the years the findings reported that aggression grew among boys, but not among girls, who watched violent shows. Eron and Huesmann reported their findings to the Office of the US Surgeon General in the 1970s and to the National Institute of Mental Health. Their findings were cited by Congress in the 1996 Telecommunications Act that put in place the V-chip requirement in later years, stating that "Studies have shown that children exposed to violent video programming at a young age have a higher tendency for violent and aggressive behavior later in life than children not so exposed."[18]

17. Leonard D. Eron and L. Rowell Huesmann, *Television and the Aggressive Child: A Cross-National Comparison* (Hillsdale, NJ: Lawrence Erlbaum Associates, 1981).
18. Fowles, *Case for Television Violence*, p. 126.

In 2000, Pulitzer Prize-winning journalist Richard Rhodes took up the media violence issue in a report entitled "The Media Violence Myth."[19] In preparing the report, Rhodes interviewed major figures in the media violence field like Eron and Huesmann, pressing them to answer critics who had questioned the validity of their findings. Eron told Rhodes of the pressures that had been put upon researchers by government officials who wanted them to find negative effects—stating that the scientists really hadn't concluded that their research proved much of a link between viewing habits and later aggression. Only a few boys seemed to have changed their habits over the years and most weren't affected at all. Heusmann later admitted that the "proof" in the study that had fueled so much fervor and resulted in legislative action was derived from a handful of boys and that he and his collaborators had never thought that media alone could be the cause of antisocial behavior. Huesmann has "deliberately misrepresented his findings," Rhodes charges. Huesmann has claimed that there is a strong relationship between "early violence viewing and later criminality." Yet his conclusion was based on only three cases among 145 adult males who watched action television shows as children.

"There's no evidence that mock violence makes people violent, and there's some evidence that it makes them more peaceful," Rhodes concludes.[20] Rhodes is also critical of the work of Brandon Centerwall, another scientist whose studies are frequently cited by legislators and other advocates of restricting media violence.[21] Centerwall, a psychiatrist whose research was a mainstay of the Senate Judiciary Committee's 1999 report,

19. Richard Rhodes, "The Media Violence Myth," *New York Times*, Op-Ed page, September 17, 2000.
20. Ibid.
21. US Senate Committee on the Judiciary, *Children, Violence, and the Media: A Report for Parents and Policy Makers* (September 14, 1999), in Louise I. Gerdes, ed., *Media Violence: Opposing Viewpoints* (San Diego, CA: Greenhaven, 2004), http://commdocs.house.gov /committees/judiciary/. Accessed October 11, 2005.

"Children, Violence and the Media: A Report for Parents and Policy Makers," claims that the introduction of television doubles the violent crime rate. Rhodes cites evidence showing that violent crime rates in Europe and Japan either stayed the same or declined in the years following the introduction of television. Rhodes argues that Centerwall's theory is also contradicted by falling US crimes rates despite continuing and even increased exposure to media.

> *"Our estimates suggest that in the short run, violent movies deter almost 1,000 assaults on an average weekend."*

Does Movie Violence Increase Violent Crime?

Gordon Dahl and Stefano DellaVigna

Gordon Dahl is an associate professor of economics at the University of California, San Diego; Stefano DellaVigna is an associate professor of economics at the University of California, Berkeley. In the following viewpoint, they argue that violent movies tend to reduce violent crime. They say this is because more violent groups, especially young men, choose to attend violent movies, which prevents them from committing violent acts. The authors note that movie attendance also prevents attendees from drinking alcohol. Since alcohol is linked to violent crime, they say, the reduction of alcohol use also decreases violent crime.

As you read, consider the following questions:

1. What do the authors give as an example of a strongly violent movie, a mildly violent movie, and a nonviolent movie?

2. According to the authors, what is the estimated yearly social gain in avoided victimization losses provided by violent movies?

3. Why do the authors believe that their results do not contradict laboratory experiments which show that violent movies tend to make people who watch them more violent?

Laboratory experiments in psychology find that media violence increases aggression in the short run. We analyze whether media violence affects violent crime in the field. We exploit variation in the violence of blockbuster movies from 1995 to 2004, and study the effect on same-day assaults. We find that violent crime decreases on days with larger theater audiences for violent movies. The effect is partly due to voluntary incapacitation: between 6 P.M. and 12 A.M., a one million increase in the audience for violent movies reduces violent crime by 1.1% to 1.3%. After exposure to the movie, between 12 A.M. and 6 A.M., violent crime is reduced by an even larger percent. This finding is explained by the self-selection of violent individuals into violent movie attendance, leading to a substitution away from more volatile activities. In particular, movie attendance appears to reduce alcohol consumption. The results emphasize that media exposure affects behavior not only via content, but also because it changes time spent in alternative activities. The substitution away from more dangerous activities in the field can explain the differences with the laboratory findings. Our estimates suggest that in the short run, violent movies deter almost 1,000 assaults on an average weekend. Although our design does not allow us to estimate long-run effects, we find no evidence of medium-run effects up to three weeks after initial exposure.

I. Introduction

Does media violence trigger violent crime? This question is important for both policy and scientific research. In 2000, the

Federal Trade Commission issued a report at the request of the president and the Congress, surveying the scientific evidence and warning of negative consequences. In the same year, the American Medical Association, together with five other public-health organizations, issued a joint statement on the risks of exposure to media violence (American Academy of Pediatrics et al. 2000).

The evidence cited in these reports, surveyed by Anderson and Buschman (2001) and Anderson et al. (2003), however, does not establish a causal link between media violence and violent crime. The experimental literature exposes subjects in the laboratory (typically children or college students) to short, violent video clips. These experiments find a sharp increase in aggressive behavior immediately after the media exposure, compared to a control group exposed to nonviolent clips. This literature provides causal evidence on the short-run impact of media violence on aggressiveness, but not whether this translates into higher levels of violent crime in the field. A second literature (e.g., Johnson et al. [2002]) shows that survey respondents who watch more violent media are substantially more likely to be involved in self-reported violence and crime. This second type of evidence, although indeed linking media violence and crime, has the standard problems of endogeneity and reverse causation.

In this paper, we provide causal evidence on the short-run effect of media violence on violent crime. We exploit the natural experiment induced by time-series variation in the violence of movies shown in the theater. As in the psychology experiments, we estimate the short-run effect of exposure to violence, but unlike in the experiments, the outcome variable is violent crime rather than aggressiveness. Importantly, the laboratory and field setups also differ due to self-selection and the context of violent media exposure.

Using a violence rating system from kids-in-mind.com and daily revenue data, we generate a daily measure of national-level box-office audience for strongly violent (e.g., *Hannibal*), mildly violent (e.g., *Spider-Man*), and nonviolent movies (e.g., *Runaway Bride*). Because blockbuster movies differ significantly in violence rating, and movie sales are concentrated in the initial weekends after release, there is substantial variation in exposure to movie violence over time. The audience for strongly violent and mildly violent movies, respectively, is as high as 12 million and 25 million people on some weekends, and is close to 0 on others (see Figures 1a and 1b). We use crime data from the National Incident Based Reporting System (NIBRS) and measure violent crime on a given day as the sum of reported assaults (simple or aggravated) and intimidation.

We find that, on days with a high audience for violent movies, violent crime is lower, even after controlling flexibly for seasonality. To rule out unobserved factors that contemporaneously increase movie attendance and decrease violence, such as rainy weather, we use two strategies. First, we add controls for weather and days with high TV viewership. Second, we instrument for movie audience using the predicted movie audience based on the following weekend's audience. This instrumental variable strategy exploits the predictability of the weekly decrease in attendance. Adding in controls and instrumenting, the correlation between movie violence and violent crime becomes more negative and remains statistically significant.

The estimated effect of exposure to violent movies is small in the morning or afternoon hours (6 A.M.–6 P.M.), when movie attendance is minimal. In the evening hours (6 P.M.–12 A.M.), instead, we detect a significant negative effect on crime. For each million people watching a strongly or mildly violent movie, respectively, violent crimes decrease by 1.3% and 1.1%. The effect is smaller and statistically insignificant for nonviolent movies. In the nighttime hours following the movie showing (12 A.M.–6 A.M.), the delayed effect of exposure to movie violence is even more negative. For each million people watching a strongly or mildly violent movie, respectively, violent crime decreases by 1.9% and 2.1%. Nonviolent movies have no statistically significant impact.

Unlike in the psychology experiments, therefore, media violence appears to decrease violent behavior in the immediate aftermath of exposure, with large aggregate effects. The total net effect of violent movies is to decrease assaults by roughly 1,000 occurrences per weekend, for an annual total of about 52,000 weekend assaults prevented. This translates into an estimated yearly social gain of approximately $695 million in avoided victimization losses (direct monetary costs plus intangible quality-of-life costs). The results are robust to a variety of alternative specifications, measures of movie violence, instrument sets, and placebo tests. Additional estimates using variation in violent DVD and VHS video rentals are consistent with our main findings.

We also examine the delayed impact of exposure to movie violence on violent crime. Although our research design (like the laboratory designs) cannot test for a long-run impact, we can examine the medium-run impact in the days and weeks following exposure. We find no impact on violent crime on Monday and Tuesday following weekend movie exposure. We also find no impact one, two, and three weeks after initial exposure, controlling for current exposure. Hence, the same-day decrease in crime is unlikely to be due to intertemporal substitution of crime from the following days.

To interpret the results, we develop a simple model where utility-maximizing consumers choose between violent movies, nonviolent movies, and an alternative activity. These options generate violent crime at different rates. The model provides three main insights. First, in the reduced form implied by the model, the estimates of exposure to violent movies capture the impact for the self-selected population that chooses to attend violent movies, and not the population at large. In particular, the violent subpopulation self-selects into more violent movies, magnifying any effects of exposure. Second, the reduced-form estimates capture the net effect of watching a violent movie and not participating in the next-best alternative activity. A blockbuster violent movie has a direct effect on crime as more indi-

Weekend Theater Audience of Strongly Violent Movies, January 1995–July 2004

Plot of weekend (Friday through Sunday) box-office audience in millions of people for movies rated as strongly violent. The ten weekends with the highest audience for strongly violent movies are labeled. Movies are rated as strongly violent if they have a kids-in -mind.com rating 8–10. The audience data are from box-office sales (from the-numbers.com) deflated by the average price of a ticket.

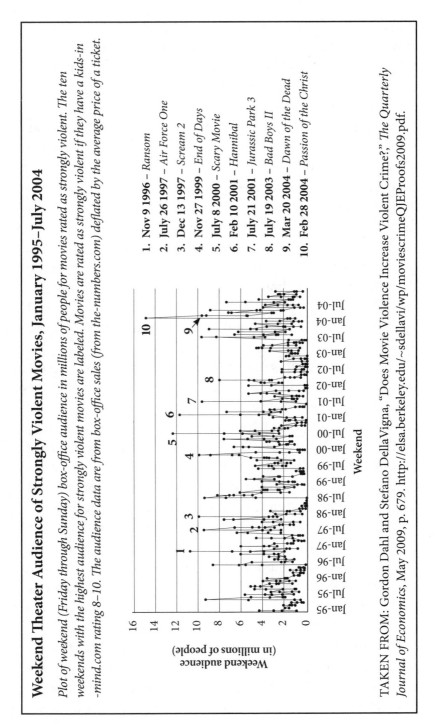

1. Nov 9 1996 – *Ransom*
2. July 26 1997 – *Air Force One*
3. Dec 13 1997 – *Scream 2*
4. Nov 27 1999 – *End of Days*
5. July 8 2000 – *Scary Movie*
6. Feb 10 2001 – *Hannibal*
7. July 21 2001 – *Jurassic Park 3*
8. July 19 2003 – *Bad Boys II*
9. Mar 20 2004 – *Dawn of the Dead*
10. Feb 28 2004 – *Passion of the Christ*

TAKEN FROM: Gordon Dahl and Stefano DellaVigna, "Does Movie Violence Increase Violent Crime?," *The Quarterly Journal of Economics*, May 2009, p. 679. http://elsa.berkeley.edu/~sdellavi/wp/moviescrimeQJEProofs2009.pdf.

viduals are exposed to screen violence, but also an indirect effect as people are drawn away from an alternative activity (such as drinking at a bar) and its associated level of violence. Third, it is possible to identify the direct effect of violent movies if one can account for self-selection.

We interpret the first empirical result, that exposure to violent movies lowers same-day violent crime in the evening (6 P.M. to 12 A.M.), as voluntary incapacitation. On evenings with high attendance at violent movies, potential criminals choose to be in the movie theater and hence are incapacitated from committing crimes. The incapacitation effect is larger for violent movies because potential criminals self-select into violent, rather than nonviolent, movies. Indeed, using data from the Consumer Expenditure Survey time diaries, we document substantial self-selection. Demographic groups with higher crime rates, such as young men, select disproportionately into watching violent movies.

The second result is that violent movies lower violent crime in the night after exposure (12 A.M. to 6 A.M.). These estimates reflect the difference between the direct effect of movie violence and the violence level associated with an alternative activity. Hence, the reduction in crime associated with violent movies is best understood as movie attendance displacing more volatile alternative activities both during and after movie attendance. Because alcohol is a prominent factor that has been linked to violent crime (Carpenter and Dobkin, 2009), and alcohol is not served in movie theaters, one potential mechanism is a reduction in alcohol consumption associated with movie attendance. Consistent with this mechanism, we find larger decreases for assaults involving alcohol or drugs and for assaults committed by offenders just over (versus just under) the legal drinking age.

A common theme to the findings above is the importance of self-selection of potential criminals into violent movies. We provide additional evidence on selection using ratings data from the Internet Movie Database (IMDb). We categorize movies based on how frequently they are rated by young males. We find that, even after controlling for the level of violence, movies that disproportionately attract young males significantly lower violent crime.

Our second result appears to contradict the evidence from laboratory experiments, which find that violent movies increase aggression through an arousal effect. However, the field and laboratory results are not necessarily contradictory. The laboratory experiments estimate the impact of violent movies in partial equilibrium, holding the alternative activities constant. Our natural experiment instead allows individuals to decide in equilibrium between a movie and an alternative activity. Exposure to movie violence can lower violent behavior relative to the foregone alternative activity (the field findings), even if it increases violent behavior relative to exposure to nonviolent movies (the laboratory findings). Under assumptions that allow us to estimate the amount of selection, our field estimates can be used to infer the effect of exposure, holding the alternative activities constant (as in the laboratory).

> "The portrayal of torture in popular culture is having a significant impact on how interrogations are conducted in the field. U.S. soldiers are imitating the techniques they have seen on television."

Media Influence Has Led to Public Acceptance of Torture

Maura Moynihan

In the following viewpoint, author and journalist Maura Moynihan argues that portrayals of torture on television and in advertising have desensitized Americans to torture. In particular, she singles out media campaigns by the George W. Bush administration, the television drama Dexter *about a serial killer, and fashion shows in which models were dressed as torture victims. Moynihan argues that these media images make torture by the US government more politically popular and damage society.*

As you read, consider the following questions:

1. According to UCLA's Television Monitoring Project, how have the characters who torture on television changed in recent years?

2. What advertising campaigns does Moynihan point to as including torture imagery?

3. How does the Human Rights Watch believe images of torture will affect the United States' image around the world?

In his first days in office [in early 2009], President Barack Obama took a pen and signed executive orders halting the use of torture, shutting Guantanamo [a US prison in Guantanamo Bay, Cuba, which has been criticized for failing to give inmates due process] and banning secret CIA [Central Intelligence Agency] prisons overseas, as he vowed to fight terrorism "in a manner that is consistent with our values and our ideals."

The Popularity of Torture

Shortly thereafter, a poll showed that Americans did not overwhelmingly support the president's rejection of the [George W.] Bush administration's use of torture as an instrument of the state.

In their zeal to legalize torture and trounce the Bill of Rights, the Bush team crafted a media campaign to sell the "War on Terror" as a righteous quest retribution for 9/11 [2001 terrorist attacks] inciting fear of future carnage to justify violating the Geneva protocols [international agreements banning torture] and the U.S. Army Field Manual. While the Bush torture policy made stunning progress through the courts and the legislature, with the Patriot Act [of 2001, which gave broad powers to the government] and the Military Commissions Act of 2006 [which authorized trials by military commissions rather than courts]; there followed an increase in the normalization of torture images in popular culture, a growing acceptance of violence as effective, routine.

When photographs of torture and abuse at Abu Ghraib [a US military prison in Iraq] appeared in 2004, Bush's approval ratings sank, yet torture themes multiplied in film and TV. From 2002 through 2005, the Parents Television Council counted 624 torture scenes in prime time, a six-fold increase. [University of

24 and the US Army

U.S. Army Brigadier General Patrick Finnegan, disturbed by the effect that [the television show] *24* was having on future soldiers, traveled to California in 2006 to meet with the producers, hoping to persuade them to consider the consequences of their portrayal of [hero] Jack Bauer and the constant success of his barbaric [torture] techniques. Instead, he hoped to see a story line where torture backfires, because the unfailing success of Jack's methods was encouraging support from U.S. soldiers for the use of torture.

Sara E. Quay and Amy M. Damico,
September 11 in Popular Culture: A Guide.
Santa Barbara, CA: ABC-CLIO, 2010, p. 146.

California's] UCLA's Television Violence Monitoring Project reports "torture on TV shows is significantly higher than it was five years ago and the characters who torture have changed. It used to be that only villains on television tortured. Today, "good guy" and heroic American characters torture—and this torture is depicted as necessary, effective and even patriotic."

Primetime Torture

Human Rights First has just released a short film entitled "Primetime Torture" that examines how torture and interrogation scenes are portrayed in television programming. A retired military leader interviewed for the film says, "The portrayal of torture in popular culture is having a significant impact on how interrogations are conducted in the field. U.S. soldiers are imitating the techniques they have seen on television—because they think such tactics work."

Lately it seems that three out of five offerings at the local Cineplex are tales of clever and nimble torturers and serial killers. This mass marketing of the murderer, sadist and child molester endows the deviant with a fictitious intelligence [and] the pretense of a rich and complex "inner life," a particularly annoying Hollywood buzzword. Such characters aren't presented as perverts, rather, they're complex geniuses, creative and tormented, ever misunderstood. It must come from the suits, who study box office returns for the "Texas Chainsaw Massacre" franchise. Whereas actresses frequently complain that the only roles available are for killers or tarts, actors bemoan the dearth of "serious" movies amid piles of scripts about guys shooting off guns. They'll play the killer if they have to, it's work.

Showtime has launched a hit series called *Dexter*, "America's Favorite Serial Killer; He's Got A Way with Murder." The star, Michael C. Hall, has become a pin-up icon in men's magazines, where he speaks rapturously in interviews about the joys of portraying "a serial killer with a conscience," in that he only kills bad people, or anyone he finds irritating. There's a Dexter screensaver, board game and Facebook site, where you can "Dexterize" your friend's profile. Huh?

In the Bush years torture images migrated from Hollywood to fashion and advertising. Last season a TV commercial featuring lesbian-bondage-torture imagery got heavy rotation on prime time. A sleek and luscious model is strapped to a restraining chair, encircled by another model wielding a hair dryer like a weapon, whilst growling, "In." A new color print ad in women's magazines shows a ferocious swat team breaking into a bathroom, hoisting bottles of toilet bowl cleaner like clubs. I guess it's supposed to make you feel "safe."

Torture Chic

In 2007 a fashion blog proclaimed: "Torture is the New Black," when John Galliano's 2007 runway show male models wore hoods, nooses, handcuffs, and had their bodies painted with gashes, cuts and cigarette burns. Then *Italian Vogue* ran 30 pages of color photographs by Steven Meisel, depicting models elegantly clad in Dolce & Gabbana, Prada and more, being interrogated and beaten by policemen with clubs, knives, guns and attack dogs. Many fashion writers embraced "Torture Chic." Joanna Bourke, a professor at Birkbeck College, observed that the images served "the interests of the politics of torture and abuse. There is a vicarious satisfaction in viewing these depictions of cruelty in the interests of national security."

Human Rights First offers . . . recommendations to "creators of popular culture who are writing scenes about interrogation." These include:

> U.S. interrogators say that not only is torture illegal and immoral; it is also ineffective as an interrogation tactic—because it is unreliable. Moreover, evidence gained through torture is inadmissible in court—and therefore unusable for prosecuting alleged terrorists or criminals.
>
> Torture, as it is performed by American characters on television, regularly produces reliable information—and quite quickly. When writing about interrogation, writers might consider creating scenes that more accurately mirror reality: showing that torture often incapacitates suspects (or kills them); that innocent people are often mistakenly tortured; or that victims of torture provide false information. On television today, torture has few consequences for the torturer and the tortured . . . it would be difficult, if not impossible, for those who torture or are tortured to resume normal life quickly as they do on television.
>
> Remember that American popular culture is exported widely around the world. . . . With the abuses at Abu Grahib and Guantanamo fresh in people's minds, exporting the glorification of torture by American military and police personnel further tarnishes America's image in the world.

Fans of *Dexter* and *24* [a television show well-known for featuring torture] have become artificially desensitized to torture, having never experienced it themselves, or seen a friend or relative whipped, burned, frozen or starved.

Daniel Patrick Moynihan once wrote: "The central conservative truth is that it is culture, not politics, that determines the success of a society. The central liberal truth is that politics can change a culture and save it from itself." In his 1993 essay "Defining Deviancy Down" he observed Americans "must be wary of normalizing social pathology that leads to trauma . . . we are getting used to a lot of behavior that isn't good for us."

| "Whereas before, torture was the 'tool of the enemy,' now torture is the tool of [TV character] Jack Bauer. Its use is a heroic act of defiance."

Government Influence Has Led to Media Acceptance of Torture

Scott Horton

In the following viewpoint, attorney Scott Horton contends that the George W. Bush administration launched a deliberate campaign to promote its torture policies. Horton says that the administration influenced news organizations and networks to suppress language or opinions that opposed torture. He says that the administration also worked with producers of the television show 24 to create deliberate pro-torture propaganda. Horton concludes that the co-optation of the media by torture proponents is dangerous for the United States. Horton is a contributing editor of Harper's and an attorney known for his work in human rights law.

As you read, consider the following questions:

1. According to Horton, how did the *New York Times* use the word "torture," and how did it avoid using the word?

2. How does Horton say Hollywood used torture during and after World War II?

3. What does Horton say are the problems with the "ticking-bomb" scenario?

In the last eighteen months [starting in late 2006], Antonin Scalia, one of the most influential judges in American history, has twice suggested that he would turn to a fictional television character named Jack Bauer to resolve legal questions about torture. The first time was in a speech in Canada, and the second, only three weeks ago [February 2008], in an interview with the BBC [the public media company in Britain]. This is evidence of the unprecedented influence of a television program on one of the most important legal policy issues before our country today. And it is, or should be, very troubling.

Most of our discussion of torture has focused on the arena of policy formation and debate. We have seen the issues tackled from the perspectives of the law, of ethics and from a utilitarian stance. That is, we have had a focus on the discussion which has occurred in Washington [DC], within the upper echelons of Government, the courts, Congress, major think tanks and the academy. But in this process we are ignoring the forum in which public opinion on these questions may well be settled: namely, in the broadcast media.

Of course, one of the most pervasive memes of our modern political experience has been the notion of the "liberal media," namely that key figures in broadcast and print media are more liberal than the average American, and that news and entertainment reflect their "liberal" bias. The torture issue provides an interesting opportunity to test this thesis. My view is that the [George W. Bush] Administration has had tremendous impact on coverage of the issue. It was able to transform well-settled media views.

There are two aspects to this industry that I want to address today—first, news and second entertainment, though there is a rather nebulous middle ground of infotainment. But I want to come to a focus on the entertainment side, where the most serious issues exist.

Torture in the News

News coverage of the torture issue began in proper terms after the publication of the Abu Ghraib photographs.[1] There were a handful of reports that predated this, such as notice of the first two deaths in Bagram Air Base.[2] At the time that the Abu Ghraib photographs appeared, I had completed a major study for the NYC Bar Association looking into legal standards governing interrogation practices. This study had been directly inspired by information the Bar had received from its JAG [Judge Advocate General; the legal branch of the armed forces] members to the effect that unlawful torture techniques were being used. Specifically, the following techniques were the focus of our concern: waterboarding, long-time standing, hypothermia, sleep deprivation in excess of two days, the use of psychotropic drugs and the sensory deprivation/sensory overload techniques first developed for the CIA at McGill University. Each of these techniques has a long history. Each had historically been condemned as "torture" by the United States when used by other nations. Each was clearly prohibited under the prior U.S. Army Field Manual. And each was now being used.

I discovered that when I gave interviews to major media on this subject, any time I used the word "torture" with reference to these techniques, the interview passage would not be used. At one point I was informed by a cable news network that "we put this on international, because we can't use *that word* on the domestic feed." "That word" was torture. I was coached or told that the words "coercive interrogation technique" were fine, but "torture" was a red light. Why? The Administration objected vehemently to the use of this word. After all, President Bush has gone before the cameras and stated more than three dozen times "We do not torture." By using the T-word, I was told, I

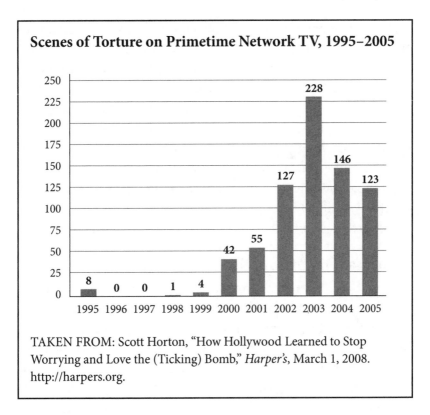

Scenes of Torture on Primetime Network TV, 1995–2005

TAKEN FROM: Scott Horton, "How Hollywood Learned to Stop Worrying and Love the (Ticking) Bomb," *Harper's*, March 1, 2008. http://harpers.org.

was challenging the honesty of the president. You just couldn't do that.

In early 2005, I took a bit of time to go through one newspaper—*The New York Times*—to examine its use of the word "torture." I found that the word "torture" was regularly used to described a neighbor who played his stereo too loud, or some similar minor nuisance. Also the word "torture" could be used routinely to describe techniques used by foreign powers which were hostile to the United States. But the style rule seemed very clear: it could not be used in reporting associated with anything the Bush Administration was doing.

In response to the scandal that Abu Ghraib produced, the Administration attempted a new gambit. It could be simply summarized as "scapegoat the grunts." Unnamed Defense Department spokesmen spoke on a not-for-attribution basis to Pentagon reporters in the weeks after the *New Yorker*'s and *60 Minutes*' publication of photographs. The unit involved was, we were told, a bunch of uneducated hillbillies from Appalachia, and economic circumstances led the Army increasingly to reach down low to bring in people with dubious backgrounds. A formal review was prepared by a team headed by former DOD [Department of Defense] Secretary James Schlesinger, which stated that all of the trouble was due to "animal house on the nightshift," a phrase which mysteriously cropped up several days before the release of the report on a number of right-wing radio talk programs.

A Formal Disinformation Campaign

Of course, Schlesinger's formulation which was spread all across the media, was at odds with the report itself, which clearly linked the problems to policies authorized and implemented by the Secretary of Defense. Schlesinger was being used as part of a formal disinformation campaign which was aggressively peddled in the media. By and large it was not believed, but it provided a sufficient cover for the Administration to hold on to its "base" of the most Conservative 40% of American voters, and saw Bush and [Vice President Dick] Cheney through the 2004 elections.

I worked with Alex Gibney, Sid Blumenthal and others in the preparation of *Taxi to the Dark Side* and I appear in the film. The objective of this exercise was to clarify in a definitive way how policies which were settled in the secretive inner sanctum of Washington defense and national security establishment were implemented in the field, and how the Administration attempted—largely through a series of rather staggering deceits—to cover this up. *Taxi* intentionally does not start with Abu Ghraib, but rather with the case of Dilawar, an Afghan taxi driver who was falsely arrested, imprisoned and brutally tortured to death. His handling was start to finish in accordance with formally approved Bush Administration policies. The film then traces the flow of these practices to and from Abu Ghraib, Camp Cropper [a US holding facility in Baghdad] and Guantánamo [a US holding facility in Cuba], and the flood of official disinformation about them. This film was prepared at the highest levels of objectivity and professionalism and the key figures who carry the dialogue are Bush Administration actors—Alberto Mora [a former general counsel of the Navy who opposed torture], Larry Wilkerson [a former chief of staff of Secretary of State Colin Powell], John Yoo [a former Department of Justice official who argued that some torture techniques were legal] and the prison guards themselves, for instance. In one video segment, a senior U.S. officer in Afghanistan speaks candidly about the orders from the Pentagon to use the brutal techniques, and to mislead about their use. We also see how a fake death certificate was issued for Dilawar and then we slowly develop the actual course of events leading to his death. More than one hundred detainees have now died in U.S. captivity, and a large part of those deaths are linked to the use of torture and other brutal interrogation techniques.

When *Taxi* was done, it was shown to broad acclaim at the Tribeca Film Festival, where it was recognized as best documentary. Discovery expressed a strong interest in the product and stepped up to acquire it. Then strange things started happening. The MPAA [Motion Picture Association of America] raised objections to the poster for the film because it showed a prisoner who was hooded, which is of course the standard practice for the US in transporting prisoners. MPAA said it had ethical reservations about showing a prisoner with a hood, that this suggested torture or abuse, and was inappropriate. Of course, that was the exact point. This was a documentary, not an entertainment piece. After weeks of wrangling the MPAA receded. Then we learned that Discovery, which had talked about transmission of the film in the spring, had decided to simply put it on the shelf. The film was "too controversial," they said. What they meant was that the White House would take offense from it.

There was a loud public outcry over this act of censorship, and the film was flipped to HBO, which will now broadcast it. When this is transmitted, American audiences will see for the first time, comprehensively, how the Bush Administration consciously introduced torture techniques in American prisons—and how it consciously lied about what it did.

The story of *Taxi* shows the sort of problems faced by anyone who wants to present an accurate and candid portrait of the Bush Administration's policies of official cruelty. But the entertainment side of the ledger is even more disturbing.

Entertainment and Torture

We should start by taking a step back in time. The theme of torture is nothing new to Hollywood, of course, it has appeared in many forms, frequently in romanticized historical settings. But when it makes its appearance in connection with contemporary settings there are some consistent themes. As the World War II era propaganda poster says "Torture—The Tool of the Enemy." We used torture to define the enemy and to separate the enemy from us. The use of torture by the enemy marked them. They were evil, intrinsically evil, because of their use of these techniques. Conversely, the victims were Americans or American allies. Torture killed or maimed, but it did not work. It was a sign of weakness. A good example of these themes and their development can be found in a series of World War II films, such as *13, rue Madeleine*, which was of course the address of the Gestapo in Paris during World War II.

This thematic approach held through the Cold War, when torture became more exotic and was presented as a still greater threat to the human spirit. Torture was an effort to crush the individual, to destroy the personality, to bend its victim to the will of the totalitarian state.

Still, torture scenes were relatively infrequent. . . .

The entertainment industry latches on to the events of the day and tries to take a ride from them. That is the simple nature of things. So the reintroduction of torture as a theme in the broadcast world was to be expected. But something happened beginning in 2002 which was a bit surprising, and that was the fairly dramatic transformation of the way in which torture was addressed by Hollywood. I will be generalizing here, and there are exceptions to every statement, but I will focus on one single program: Fox's *24*, which takes an easy first place in this process—it offers 67 torture scenes in the first five seasons. . . .

Whereas before, torture was the "tool of the enemy," now torture is the tool of Jack Bauer [the hero of *24*]. Its use is a heroic act of defiance, often of petty bureaucratic limitations, or of conceited liberals whose personal conscience means more to them than the safety of their fellow citizens. While Bauer is presented as an ultimate heroic figure (and also a figure with some heroic flaws), those who challenge use of the rough stuff are naïve, and their presence and involvement in the national security process is threatening. We see a liberal who defends a Middle Eastern neighbor then under suspicion, and who winds up being killed because the neighbor is in fact a terrorist.

We're looking at a Hollywood specialty: a "reality" show which is divorced from reality.

It grossly simplifies necessarily complex facts, and it pares away critical factors which a responsible citizen should be thinking about. But more importantly, perhaps, it is a head-on attack on morality and ethics. The critics of torture are shallow figures, self-serving politicians—vain, arrogant, indifferent to the harm they are doing to society. But in fact the arguments against torture are profound and informed by centuries of human experience and religious doctrine. Torture has in the course of the last two hundred years emerged as an intrinsic evil in Christian teaching; the teaching of most churches—Protestant, Catholic, Evangelical—rejects the idea that a state can ever legitimately employ torture.

Key to *24*'s success is the ticking bomb scenario—indeed you hear it with all the introductions, breaks and trailers—the seconds ticking off. The myth of the ticking bomb is the core of the program. Torture always works. Torture always saves the day. Torture is the ultimate act of heroism, of defiance of pointy-headed liberal morality in favor of service to the greater good, to society.

We should start with a frank question: has *24* been created with an overtly political agenda, namely, to create a more receptive public audience for the Bush Administration's torture policies? I think the answer to that question is now very clear. The answer is "yes." In "Whatever It Takes," Jane Mayer has waded through the sheaf of contacts between the show's producer, Joel Surnow, and Vice President Cheney and figures right around him. There is little ambiguity about this point, namely, if the torture system introduced after 9/11 [2001 terrorist attacks] can be traced back to a single person, it is Vice President Cheney. He pushed relentlessly for use of the tools of the "dark side," and he ruthlessly took out everyone who stood in his way. He also worked feverishly to disguise or cloak his intimate involvement in the entire process. I take it as a given that Surnow is working to develop public attitudes which are more accepting of torture and to overturn centuries-old prejudices against torture. He is a torture-enabler.

The key to achieving this objective consists of two steps. The first is to reduce the issue to something simple: Does torture work? If it does, why should we ever rule it out? Any other question will be dismissed as a moralizing quibble, not something that virile men would worry about. I call this the "Rambo approach" [referring to a violent action film series begun in 1982].

The Missing Elements

We should all be focused on the gap between reality and the world of *24*. Here are the major points I would make:

The irreality of the ticking-bomb. For one thing the fact that the ticking-bomb scenario upon which they build has never occurred in the entirety of human history. It's a malicious fiction.

The facts posited will simply never occur. But beyond this, while we are asked to keep our eye on the ticking-bomb scenario, it has nothing to do with the cases in which highly coercive techniques are actually used—look at the testimony of Steven Bradbury before the Judiciary Committee. He cited three instances in which waterboarding, an iconic torture technique, was used. None of them involved the ticking-bomb or anything like it.

The reliability of torture. The Intelligence Science Board looked at the question extensively and came to clear conclusions in December 2006. Torture does not work, they said. Indeed, one passage of their report was clearly a swipe at *24* which they said rested on a series of absurd premises. The belief that a person, once tortured, speaks the truth is ancient and very false. Torture, when applied, seems very likely to produce false intelligence upon which we rely to our own detriment. Ask [former US Secretary of State] Colin Powell. He delivered a key presentation to the Security Council in which he made the case for war against Iraq. The keystone of Powell's presentation turned on evidence taken from a man named al-Libi who was tortured and said that Iraq was busily at work on an WMD [weapons of mass destruction] program. This information, of course, was totally wrong. Al-Libi fabricated it because he knew this is just what the interrogators wanted to hear, and by saying it, they would stop torturing. It was a perfect demonstration of the tendency of torture to contaminate the intelligence gathering process with bogus data.

Containment. Can torture be introduced and used only in a highly limited set of cases, usually against cold-hearted terrorists, the worst of the worst? Is there not instead an inevitable rush to the bottom that results in any limitations being disregarded? . . .

For another, the nation's reputation in the world. Generations of Americans have fought and sacrificed to build a system of alliances around the world that provide our security bulwark. What has happened to those alliances? In country after country—including many of the nations which have historically been our tightest allies—our government's approval level is, as now in Turkey, within the margin of error. That's right. The percentage approving may actually be zero. In nation after nation and even among our own allies, we are outstripped by the world's last Stalinist [after Soviet dictator Josef Stalin] power, China. This is a very heavy price, and most of it has to do with torture policy. So torture policy erodes confidence of our community of allies in us, makes them hesitant to share intelligence, and to support us in counterterrorism and other operations. I have studied in some detail the consequences of U.S. torture policies for operations in Afghanistan and Iraq, where it is clear that allies are dropping out and losing enthusiasm for supporting operations, and torture policies provide the single most important motivator in this process.

Damage to military morale and discipline. George Washington was famous for his opposition to torture. He came to his views not for idealistic but for practical reasons. During the French and Indian Wars he observed brutal tactics being used in the wilderness, and he saw that the soldiers who used them were bad soldiers—disorderly, poorly disciplined, impossible to control. He concluded that torture destroyed morale and discipline. And that continues to be the accepted wisdom of the military today, and the force behind the historically unprecedented opposition of military leaders to Bush Administration policy that we saw in the winter of 2006–07. The dean of the U.S. Military Academy at West Point, BG Patrick Finnegan, visited the writers of *24* to present a complaint. This program was actually corrupting military intelligence and discipline. Soldiers in the field reach to the techniques employed by Jack Bauer—if he can use them, why can't we?

And the weightiest link in this chain tied around our national neck should be considered last. As my friend Mark Danner writes, if you assembled a team of Madison Avenue's most brilliant thinkers in a room and asked them to concoct a recruitment plan for al Qaeda [a radical Islamic terrorist organization] and its allies, we'd never come anywhere close to the one that the Bush Administration delivered up to them with the torture program. It's the major reason why today, six years after the start of the war on terror, the National Intelligence Estimate tells us that al Qaeda is back up or has exceeded the strength it had on 9/11, and the Taliban [an Islamic insurgent group in Afghanistan] has also been able to regroup and recharge, destabilizing a friendly government in Afghanistan.

The Values of 24

The current [2008] season of 24 set to begin shortly features a senate investigation looking into Jack Bauer. A Senator is out after our hero, but he defends himself brilliantly and in the end, the senate committee, we are told, sees the light and comes to understand Bauer's heroic qualities, including his willingness to use torture.

America today is witnessing something like the experience of France during the Algerian conflict [of 1952–1962, in which Algeria fought for independence from France]. [Author] Albert Camus noted and developed this carefully over a period of many years in his *Chroniques algériennes*. He saw a polarized society in France, between conservatives, traditional liberals and the Left. But there was no constituency to oppose torture. The Right embraced the cause of the colonials, and justified their reach to harsh tactics. First this was justified by arguments that the barbarity of the people justified treating them in ways that in Europe could not be countenanced. (This was an echo of arguments that [Alexis de] Tocqueville examined a century earlier in the first Algerian war.) But this wasn't a satisfying basis for a society built on liberty, equality and fraternity. So the second justification was more appealing, and it was the ticking-bomb. Camus notes that the Left also could not muster arguments against torture. It was then still in the embrace of Stalinism, which had taken with relish to the same techniques. Who remained to make the moral and social argument? Camus did. He puts it powerfully near the conclusion of that book.

> Though it may be true that, at least in history, values, be they of a nation or of humanity as a whole, do not survive unless we fight for them, neither combat (nor force) can alone suffice to justify them. Rather it must be the other way: the fight must be justified and guided by those values. We must fight for the truth and we must take care not to kill it with the very weapons we use in its defense; it is at this doubled price that we must pay in order that our words assume once more their proper power.

This is the fundamental dilemma that *24* dodges. What are the values for which Jack Bauer is fighting? Is he not abdicating them by his conduct? I am not advocating censoring of *24*. But it is critical that *24* begin to present this vitally complex and important social issue in a mature, responsible way. Right now, it is multiplying our problems.

Notes

1. In 2004 photographs of US soldiers torturing Iraqis in the Abu Ghraib prison in Iraq caused a worldwide scandal.
2. Bagram Air Base is the main detention facility for those captured by US forces in Afghanistan. There have been reports that two detainees were beaten to death there in 2002.

"In 2003, Ryan Halligan, a 13-year-old Vermont boy, hanged himself after being the target of brutal instant messages."

Cyberbullying Is a Serious Problem for Youth

Brian Fraga

In the following viewpoint, reporter Brian Fraga writes that cyberbullying is a growing and serious problem among young people. Officials say that young people are more verbally aggressive and abusive online than they would be face-to-face. Through MySpace, Facebook, and instant messaging, students have new opportunities to harass and intimidate each other, Fraga says. He concludes that cyberbullying can be extremely traumatic for students and can cause serious harm. Fraga is a crime reporter for Massachusetts' South Coast Today.

As you read, consider the following questions:

1. According to Fraga, what fraction of teens have been victimized online, and what fraction of youth have written mean or hurtful things online?

2. What does Fraga say are the most common forms of cyberbullying?

3. Why are girls especially vulnerable to cyberbullying, according to Fraga?

Bullying has moved beyond the playground and the school hallway, following young people to the realm where they spend a greater portion of their time: cyberspace.

A New Dimension of Bullying

In "cyberbullying," the name-calling, rumor-spreading and intimidation tactics take on new dimensions—and consequences— thanks to a generation of teens and pre-teens who have grown up with computers, the Internet and cell phones.

Kids today often slam each other via nasty text messages. They post mean-spirited comments on social networking sites such as MySpace and Facebook. The more tech-savvy youths spread doctored photos of other students and can even build entire Web sites to defame specific individuals.

"This is not the simple schoolyard bullying. This is peer pressure beyond belief," said Linda M. Pacheco, the director of public safety education for the Bristol County [Massachusetts] Sheriff's Department.

Cyberbullying results in many youths feeling alienated and helpless. Some have even committed suicide. Most teens will never tell their parents, who generally are clueless about what their children are going through.

"The problem is huge. The biggest concern for the most part is that parents are not aware of this," said Pacheco, who gives presentations on Internet safety in schools throughout the region. She also offers evening online safety classes for parents.

Various studies indicate that a third to almost half of teens have been victimized online. Meanwhile, nearly half of youths admit to writing mean or hurtful things to another person while online.

"It's an issue that causes real headaches for the schools and is really disruptive to the classroom environment," said Kevin Lee, the Dartmouth [MA] youth advocate.

Cyberbullying has become such an issue that the Plymouth [MA] and Bristol county district attorneys earlier this year [2009] announced a joint effort to provide, free of charge, an anti-cyberbullying computer game to all schools in both counties.

The program also was spearheaded by Raynham [MA] Police Chief Louis J. Pacheco, who has expertise in Internet crimes. Pacheco said cyberbullying is rampant, and often spills out into real-world confrontations in the streets and school grounds.

"It's the same dynamic involved in road rage," Pacheco said.

"People think they can anonymously do things in their car that they wouldn't do face-to-face. So you get these kids going off and saying things they would never say in person. Then it escalates."

Tragic Consequences

Sometimes there are tragic consequences. In 2003, Ryan Halligan, a 13-year-old Vermont boy, hanged himself after being the target of brutal instant messages. Last year in Florida, six teenage girls videotaped themselves assaulting another girl. The assailants threatened to put the video online. The fight began from text messages and comments the victim reportedly had posted on MySpace.

"Kids are so wired electronically and are so much more savvy than the adults," said Denise Gaudette, the current director of an alcohol prevention program for the New Bedford Public Schools [in MA]. Gaudette previously led school projects on violence prevention, including bullying.

"It's certainly a serious problem with the explosion of social networking sites and just the devices kids are carrying around," she said. "They have the ability to communicate so readily."

That bullying is occurring more often on the Internet makes sense given that is where youths today socialize and gossip.

Recent Incidents of Cyberbullying

In 2006, a 12-year-old seventh grader and her older sisters received hateful and threatening e-mails referencing their race and the KKK [Ku Klux Klan] and threatening physical violence against them. One line from an e-mail stated, "All I got to say is that you better watch every move you make N----- and you can tell all of your older sister(s) the KKK will be after them (too) B----." According to the family, the youngest daughter has been in counseling, dislikes school, has suffered from a great deal of emotional stress, and wishes she could just disappear.

In 2007, national and international news covered the story of Megan Meier. The 13-year-old eighth grader from a small town in Missouri committed suicide in 2006 after being harassed on MySpace by someone she thought was a 16-year-old boy named Josh Evans.

In 2008, six teenaged girls were arrested for kidnapping and assault after videotaping themselves beating a female classmate. They intended to upload the video to the Internet. Allegedly, the victim had made comments about the girls on MySpace.

Sameer Hinduja and Justin W. Patchin,
Bullying Beyond the Schoolyard: Preventing
and Responding to Cyberbullying. *Thousand
Oaks, CA: Corwin Press, 2009, p. 6.*

"This is the new mall," Pacheco said. "This is their sole means of communication, so much so that all personal connection is lost.

"They're never off-line."

The most common forms of cyberbullying are abusive Web pages and instant messages.

"It can be brutal on MySpace," Lee said.

On the social networking sites, some youths will write comments and blogs attacking other students. Teens also have been known to set up fake profiles purportedly belonging to a specific individual, only to post defamatory content and unflattering pictures.

"I've seen cases where a girl's head was Photoshopped onto a nude body and sent out to everybody in her school," Pacheco said. "The girl had to leave the school because she was so embarrassed."

"It's so crazy. You can make up any online profile and say basically anything you want," said Kellie Sicard, 17, a Dartmouth High School junior who is part of a mentoring program for freshmen.

Youths also have gained access to others' MySpace and Facebook accounts because their friends had given them their passwords and pin numbers. When the friendships soured, the teens used the information to publicly embarrass others.

Closely related is the fact that many pre-teens and teens post provocative pictures of themselves online. Even if they designate the pictures "private" so that only friends can see them, there is still a strong likelihood that the photo will get out, and be distributed among dozens, if not hundreds or thousands, of other youths.

"The stuff you find online is outrageous," Pacheco said.

"Stop and Think"

According to studies conducted by the Massachusetts Aggression Reduction Center at Bridgewater State College, the most common motives for cyberbullying are anger and the belief that cyberbullying is a joke.

Youths who are angry often do not think before they send a bitter text message or type an attacking e-mail and instant message to someone. Once the electronic message is sent, there is no way to retract it, and the damage is done.

"Before they post things online, they need to stop and think, 'Who's going to see this?'" Pacheco said.

Another reason for cyberbullying is that many youths are not aware how serious it can be. Teens generally do not know they can be charged with criminal harassment and stalking for sending intimidating electronic messages.

"It's sort of like years ago when there were kids hanging out on the street corner, someone passed by and one of them said a mean-spirited comment," Lee said. "They don't give it much thought, yet they cause much harm to certain kids."

Especially vulnerable are girls, who often have their self-esteem attacked through insults on their looks, weight and social status. The sad reality is that their tormentors are often other girls, officials said.

"Girls go after the emotional jugular. They're worse than the boys," Pacheco said.

"My experience is that it's more prevalent among girls," Lee said. "They are more susceptible to the effects of cyberbullying. Plus, girls are frequently online more than the boys."

Many victims, unsure how to cope with being attacked online, retreat into a shell and become hesitant to reach out to their parents.

"Victims do suffer in silence," Pacheco said. "There is a degree of embarrassment, confusion, not having the maturity to handle this kind of problem.

"Education will empower them to handle these extreme situations."

Meanwhile, Dartmouth High school mentors Sicard and Lauren Beaudoin do their part to improve the atmosphere in their school.

"I think by us reaching out and checking up on the new kids helps to cut down on the bullying," said Beaudoin, 18, a senior.

There are several online resources for adults and parents to educate themselves on cyberbullying and practical steps they can take to protect their children.

One of the more popular sites is iSafe.org, a nonprofit group that provides an online safety curriculum for students in Grades K–12.

The most commonly cited prevention tips advise that victims do not open messages from cyberbullies; that they block bullies from their buddy lists; save the messages in case legal action is later needed; and tell a trusted adult if they are being bullied.

"It's necessary that the adults learn more about the technology they're providing to their children," Pacheco said.

> "Research has . . . shown that kids who
> do get into trouble online are the same
> kids who get in trouble offline."

The Problems of Online Predation and Cyberbullying Have Been Exaggerated

Larry Magid

In the following viewpoint, technology analyst Larry Magid maintains that fears of online predation and cyberbullying are often exaggerated. He says that drunk driving is much more of a threat to young people than Internet harassment or cyberbullying. Magid also argues that kids who take risks online are the same ones who take risks offline. He concludes that parents need to be careful about online safety but should keep the dangers in perspective. Magid is a technology analyst for CBS News and co-author of MySpace Unraveled: A Parents Guide to Teen Social Networking.

As you read, consider the following questions:

1. What statistics does Magid cite to demonstrate the dangers of drunk driving to young people?
2. According to Magid, why is it misleading to claim that

one in five children have been sexually solicited by a
predator?

3. What percentage of youth were harassed online in the past
year, and by whom, according to NetFamilyNews.org?

A survey of 1,000 moms of teenagers commissioned by Mc-
Afee and conducted by Harris Interactive reached the surprising conclusion that "about two-thirds of mothers of teens
in the United States are just as, or more, concerned about their
teenagers' online safety, such as from threatening emails or solicitation by online sexual predators, as they are about drunk driving (62 per cent) and experimenting with drugs (65 per cent)."

That might be how moms feel, but it's not reflective of the
real world. While moms have good reason to be concerned about
how their teens use the Internet, online dangers pale compared
to the risks of drunk driving. In 2007, 6,552 people were killed
in auto accidents involving young drivers (16–20), according to
the National Highway Transportation Safety Administration. In
2006, nearly a fifth of the 7,643 15- to 20-year-old drivers involved in fatal traffic crashes had a blood alcohol concentration
of .08 or higher.

Perceptions and Reality

Perception of Internet danger has been heightened thanks to
the TV show *To Catch a Predator* and inaccurate reports stating
that "one in five children have been sexually solicited by a predator." That statistic is a misquote from a 2000 study by the Crimes
Against Children Research Center [CCRC]. The data (which,
based on a 2005 follow-up study, was revised to one in seven)
is based on a survey that asked teens if they had in the last year
received an unwanted sexual solicitation.

But many—possibly most—of those solicitations were from
other teens, not from adult predators. What's more, most recipi-
ents didn't view them as serious or threatening. "Almost all youth

handled the solicitations easily and effectively" and "extremely few youth (two out of 1,500 interviewed) were actually sexually victimized by someone they met online," reported the authors of the study.

Other studies have shown that "the stereotype of the Internet child molester who uses trickery and violence to assault children is largely inaccurate." In a survey of law enforcement investigators of Internet sex crimes, it was reported that only 5 percent of offenders pretended to be teens when trying to meet potential victims online.

Kids Have Similar Behaviors Online and Offline

Research has also shown that kids who do get into trouble online are the same kids who get in trouble offline. Most kids are pretty careful when it comes to Internet safety but a small percentage of teens take unnecessary risks that could lead to sexual solicitations and other dangers. Based on what we know about teenage risk taking, it is likely that the same kids who are abusing drugs or driving while under the influence are the same ones who are taking extraordinary risks online

Still, even among those kids, the odds of them dying, being injured or being sexually molested is quite low.

I'm not surprised by another finding in the McAfee/Harris survey that "20% of teens have engaged in cyberbullying behaviors, including posting mean or hurtful information or embarrassing pictures, spreading rumors, publicizing private communications, sending anonymous e-mails or cyberpranking someone." That number tracks other surveys on the subject, though it's important to point out that cyber bullying, while real, is also subject to exaggeration.

As reported by NetFamilyNews.org, a CCRC study of online bullying found that "9% of youth were harassed online in the past year, 43% of them by known peers and 57% by people they met online and did not know in person. . . . Most online harassment incidents did not appear to meet the standard denti of bullying used in school-based research and requiring aggression, repetition, and power imbalance."

I'm not suggesting that parents have nothing to worry about when it comes to the Internet. Parents should talk with their kids about Internet safety and engage in frequent conversations about how they behave online. But let's keep things in perspective and not turn parental concern into unjustified fears.

Periodical and Internet Sources Bibliography

The following articles have been selected to supplement the diverse views presented in this chapter.

Donah Boyd and Alice Marwick — "Bullying as True Drama," *New York Times*, September 22, 2011. www.nytimes.com.

Neal Desai, Andre Pineda, Majken Runquist, and Mark Fusunyan — "Torture at Times: Waterboarding in the Media," Harvard Kennedy School, April 2010. www.hks .harvard.edu.

Jan Hoffman — "As Bullies Go Digital, Parents Play Catch-Up," *New York Times*, December 4, 2010. www.nytimes .com.

L. Rowell Huesmann — "Nailing the Coffin Shut on Doubts that Violent Video Games Stimulate Aggression: Comment on Anderson et al.," *Psychological Bulletin*, vol. 136, no. 2, March 2010, pp. 179–181.

Jason Linkins — "Teenagers Now Look Favorably on Torture Because the Media Taught Them It Was Morally Acceptable," *Huffington Post*, April 13, 2011. www.huffingtonpost.com.

Rory O'Connor — "Media Torture," *Huffington Post*, May 12, 2009. www.huffingtonpost .com.

Rahul Parikh — "Our Overblown Paranoia About the Internet and Teens," *Salon*, May 16, 2011. www.salon.com.

Kim Sengupta — "'24', A Diplomatic Row and a Spy Chief's Lecture on Torture," *Independent*, March 11, 2010. www.independent.co.uk.

UMNews — "Expert Alert: Cyberbullying Has Many Facets, U of M Expert Says," October 13, 2010. www1 .umn.edu.

CHAPTER 2

How Should Media Violence Be Regulated?

Chapter Preface

Popular music often includes violent or sexual content that many adults believe is inappropriate for children. In order to address this issue, the Recording Industry Association of America (RIAA), under pressure from advocacy groups, agreed in the 1980s to put an explicit content parental advisory label on albums that included inappropriate content. This label was a voluntary step. Like the movie rating system, it was imposed by the industry itself, not by the government.

The creation of the parental advisory labels in the mid-1980s was very controversial. Musician Frank Zappa made a statement to Congress in which he declared that the labeling would result in "the reduction of all American music, recorded and live, to the intellectual level of a Saturday morning cartoon."

However, the RIAA system has prompted much less debate in recent years. Part of the reason is because the RIAA system is not very strict, especially compared to the movie rating system. As Tom Cole writes in an October 29, 2010, article on the NPR blog *The Record*, "Movie rating is de facto mandatory." Movies are rated by an independent board, and theaters will not show a movie that is unrated. Music, on the other hand, is rated by the artists themselves and by their record labels. There is no one standard for rating an album.

Nonetheless, the RIAA system has led to some restrictions. Certain stores, such as Wal-Mart, will not stock albums with parental advisory labels, and Apple has begun putting explicit content notices directly onto songs downloaded through its iTunes store. In a June 2, 2011, article in the *Guardian* Mark Sweeney reports that YouTube, the online video site, and Spotify, a song service, were both going to start posting notices of explicit music content "following recent concern about the amount of risqué music content too easily available to children online."

The viewpoints in the following chapter further examine the way in which violence in media is regulated by the government, industry, and parents.

> "We find that Congress could impose time channeling restrictions on excessively violent television programming in a constitutional manner."

Television Violence Adversely Affects Children and Should Be Regulated

Federal Communications Commission

The Federal Communications Commission (FCC) is a US government agency charged with oversight of broadcast and media issues. In the following viewpoint, the commission argues that violence on television causes harm to children and that the federal government has an interest in regulating it. The Commission argues that government-mandated technology to allow parents to block their children from viewing violent content is not very effective. Ratings systems, they say, are also difficult to implement. The Commission argues that the best solution may be restricting violent programs to late-night hours when few children are awake.

"Violent Television Programming and Its Impact on Children," Federal Communications Commission, FCC 07–50, April 6, 2007.

As you read, consider the following questions:

1. According to the FCC, how much television do American children watch on average?
2. Why has the US Supreme Court said that broadcasting has fewer free speech protections than other forms of speech?
3. What evidence does the FCC provide that the V-chip technology is ineffective in regulating children's viewing of violent content on television?

Television is an integral part of the lives of American families. An average American household has the television set turned on 8 hours and 11 minutes daily, and children watch on average between two and four hours of television every day. Depending on their age, one to two thirds of children have televisions in their bedrooms. By the time most children begin the first grade, they will have spent the equivalent of three school years in front of the television set.

Violent content in television programming has been a matter of private and governmental concern and discussion almost from the beginning of television broadcasting. A broad range of television programming aired today contains such content, including, for example, cartoons, dramatic series, professional sports such as boxing, news coverage, and nature programs. The public is concerned about the amount of violent television programming available to children, with many urging action to restrict such content. . . .

Violent Programs Affect Children

We . . . find that, on balance, research provides strong evidence that exposure to violence in the media can increase aggressive behavior in children, at least in the short term. Over the course of several decades, considerable research has been undertaken to examine television's impact on children's learning and behavior. . . .

The researchers have focused on three possible harmful effects: (1) increased antisocial behavior, including imitations of aggression or negative interactions with others, (2) increased desensitization to violence, and (3) increased fear of becoming a victim of violence. Researchers have theorized that children's viewing of violent television programming may affect later behavior in three ways: (1) through observing schemas about a hostile world, (2) through scripts for social problem solving that focus on aggression, and (3) through normative beliefs that aggression is acceptable. Alternatively, exposure to violent programming may desensitize the child's innate negative emotional response to violence, thus making aggressive acts easier to commit or tolerate. . . .

Some studies find evidence of a cause-and-effect relationship between viewing televised violence by children and aggression or other changes in the behavior of the children on both a short-term and a longer-term basis. For example, Craig Anderson, a professor and former chair of the Psychology Department at Iowa State University who has conducted and published numerous "media harms" studies, asserts that research on violent television, films, video games, and music reveals "unequivocal evidence" that media violence increases the likelihood of aggressive and violent behavior in both immediate and long-term contexts. According to his analyses and assessments, media violence produces short-term effects by "increasing physiological arousal and triggering an automatic tendency to imitate observed behaviors," and exposure to media violence leads to lasting aggressive behavior and desensitizes individuals to actual violence. Anderson notes that, although certain characteristics of viewers (*e.g.*, identification with aggressive characters), social environments (*e.g.*, parental influences), and media content (*e.g.*, attractiveness of the portrayed perpetrator) can influence the degree to which media violence affects aggression, "no one is exempt from the deleterious effects of media violence."

Joanne Cantor, a professor at the University of Wisconsin-Madison, concurs and states that her research has found that children show higher levels of hostility after exposure to media violence—ranging from being in a "nasty mood" to an increased tendency to interpret a neutral comment or action as an attack. She also asserts that her studies have found that media violence makes children fearful, a condition expressed as a general sense that the world is dangerous or through nightmares and other sleep disturbances. In congressional testimony, Dale Kunkel, a professor at the University of Arizona and an expert in the field of media violence, stated, "it is well established by a compelling body of scientific evidence that television violence poses a risk of harmful effects for the child-viewer." The Children's Media Policy Coalition ("CMPC"), a group consisting of several health and child advocacy groups such as the American Academy of Pediatrics, argues that certain critics of the "cause and effect theory" have mischaracterized the numerous studies by limiting the question to whether or not "watching violence on television causes watchers to commit violence." According to CMPC, the conclusion is not that media violence is the sole cause of aggression in children, but that the depiction of violence in media is one factor potentially contributing to the risk that children will suffer a number of harmful effects. Thus, there is a considerable research community that has studied television's effects on children's health over an extended period of time and defends the proposition that viewing this programming has adverse consequences for the child audience. . . .

Restricting Violent Programming

Members of Congress asked the [Federal Communications] Commission to address the government's authority, consistent with the First Amendment [which protects freedom of speech], to restrict the broadcast or other distribution of excessively violent programming and what measures to constrain or regulate such programming are most likely to be sustained in court.

Accordingly, we discuss below regulatory alternatives for protecting children from violent television content. We begin, however, with a brief overview of the relevant constitutional framework.

Violent speech and depictions of violence have been found by the courts to be protected by the First Amendment. However, "each medium of expression presents special First Amendment problems," with broadcasting historically receiving "the most limited First Amendment protection." Thus, even when broadcast speech "lies at the heart of First Amendment protection," the government may regulate it so long as its interest in doing so is "substantial" and the restriction is "narrowly tailored" to further that interest. While a restriction on the content of protected speech will generally be upheld only if it satisfies strict scrutiny, meaning that the restriction must further a compelling government interest and be the least restrictive means to further that interest, this exacting standard does not apply to the regulation of broadcast speech.

In the realm of indecency, the U.S. Supreme Court has identified two principal reasons for the reduced First Amendment protection afforded to broadcasting: first, its "uniquely pervasive presence in the lives of all Americans"; and second, its accessibility to children, coupled with the government's interests in the well-being of children and in supporting parental supervision of children. In light of these characteristics, the Court, in *Pacifica* [a 1978 Supreme Court case], upheld the Commission's authority to regulate the broadcast of indecent material. Relying on *Pacifica*, the U.S. Court of Appeals for the District of Columbia Circuit later concluded in *ACT III* [in 1995] that the "channeling" of indecent content to the hours between 10:00 P.M. and 6:00 A.M. would not unduly burden First Amendment rights. It held that such regulation would promote the government's "compelling interest in supporting parental supervision of what children see and hear on the public airwaves." It also noted that it is "evident beyond the need for elaboration" that the government's "interest in safeguarding the physical and psychological well-being of a minor is compelling." In addition, in light of relevant U.S. Supreme Court precedent, the D.C. Circuit refused in *ACT III* to insist on scientific evidence that indecent content harms children, concluding that the government's interest in the well-being of minors is not "limited to protecting them from clinically measurable injury."

Time Channeling

Members of Congress asked the Commission to address possible measures to protect children from excessively violent television content. We begin by discussing time channeling restrictions that would restrict such programming to hours when children are less likely to be in the viewing audience. We note that commenters disagreed about the constitutionality of such requirements. [Mike] Pappas argued that they would be likely to pass constitutional muster because the government interests are substantially the same as those at stake in regulating broadcast indecency. Other commenters maintain that such requirements would be unconstitutional and unworkable.

After carefully evaluating these comments and relevant precedent, we find that Congress could impose time channeling restrictions on excessively violent television programming in a constitutional manner. Just as the government has a compelling interest in protecting children from sexually explicit programming, a strong argument can be made . . . that the government also has a compelling interest in protecting children from violent programming and supporting parental supervision of minors' viewing of violent programming. We also believe that, if properly defined, excessively violent programming, like indecent programming, occupies a relatively low position in the hierarchy of First Amendment values because it is of "slight social value as a step to truth." Such programming is entitled to reduced First Amendment protection because of its pervasiveness and accessibility to children pursuant to the U.S. Supreme Court's reasoning in *Pacifica*.

To be sure, the government, when imposing time channeling, would have to show that such regulation is a narrowly tailored means of vindicating its interests in promoting parental supervision and protecting children. In this regard, however, we note, that while the alternative measures discussed below—viewer-initiated blocking and mandatory ratings—would impose lesser burdens on protected speech, we are skeptical that they will fully serve the government's interests in promoting parental supervision and protecting the well-being of minors. In addition to these measures, as discussed below, another way of providing consumers greater control—and therefore greater ability to avoid violent programming—could be to require video channels to be offered on an "a la carte" basis. As the D.C. Circuit has noted in the context of indecency: "It is fanciful to believe that the vast majority of parents who wish to shield their children from indecent material can effectively do so without meaningful restrictions on the airing of broadcast indecency." To cite just some of the relevant data, 81 percent of children ages two through seven sometimes watch television without adult supervision, and 91 percent of children ages four through six have turned on the television by themselves. In addition, as discussed below, the studies and surveys conducted to date tend to show that blocking technologies and the associated TV ratings system are of limited effectiveness in supporting parental supervision of minors' viewing habits.

Generally, however, the sustainability of time channeling restrictions would depend on a number of specific evidentiary considerations. Therefore, should Congress wish to adopt time channeling restrictions, lawmakers should make specific findings to support such restrictions. Significant issues that Congress may wish to address include the nature of the harm to children inflicted by violent television content, how to define such content, and the ages of the children that the government is seeking to protect. For example, indecent material is channeled to the hours between 10:00 P.M. and 6:00 A.M. This "safe harbor" is based on evidence

TV Parental Guideline Ratings

TV-Y (All Children). Whether animated or live-action, the [program is] specifically designed for a very young audience, including children from ages 2–6. This program is not expected to frighten younger children.

TV-Y7 (Directed to Older Children). It may be more appropriate for children [with] the developmental skills needed to distinguish between make-believe and reality. Themes and elements in this program may include mild fantasy or comedic violence, or may frighten children under the age of 7. . . .

TV-G (General Audiencxe). Although this rating does not signify a program designed specifically for children, most parents may let younger children watch this program unattended. It contains little or no violence, no strong language and little or no sexual dialogue or situations.

TV-PG (Parental Guidance Suggested). Many parents may want to watch it with their younger children. The theme itself may call for parental guidance and/or the program contains one or more of the following: moderate violence (V), some sexual situations (S), infrequent coarse language (L), or some suggestive dialogue (D).

TV-14 (Parents Strongly Cautioned). Parents are strongly urged to exercise greater care in monitoring this program and are cautioned against letting children under the age of 14 watch unattended.

TV-MA (Mature Audience Only—may be unsuitable for children under 17). This program contains one or more of the following: graphic violence (V), explicit sexual activity (S), or crude indecent language (L).

Federal Communications Commission,
"V-Chip: Viewing Television Responsibly,"
July 8, 2003. http://transition.fcc.gov/vchip.

that children 17 years of age and under are less likely to be in the audience during these hours. With respect to violent program content, the research suggests that younger children are most at risk, possibly requiring a different conclusion as to the ages of children to be protected and the appropriate "safe harbor" hours.

Viewer-Initiated Blocking

Besides time channeling, another possible means of protecting children from violent television content is to strengthen mechanisms that enable viewer-initiated blocking of such content. In 1996, Congress amended Title III of the Communications Act to require the incorporation of blocking technology into television sets. As of January 1, 2000, all television sets manufactured in the United States or shipped in interstate commerce with a picture screen of thirteen inches or larger must be equipped with a "V-chip" system that can be programmed to block violent, sexual, or other programming that parents do not wish their children to view. However, out of a total universe of 280 million sets in U.S. households, only about 119 million sets in use today, or less than half, are equipped with V-chips.

Based on the studies and surveys conducted to date, we believe that the evidence clearly points to one conclusion: the V-chip is of limited effectiveness in protecting children from violent television content. In order for V-chip technology to block a specific category of television programming, such as violent content, it must be activated. However, many parents do not even know if the television sets in their households incorporate this technology and, of those who do, many do not use it. In 2004, the Kaiser Family Foundation conducted a telephone survey of 1,001 parents of children ages 2–17. The results showed: (1) only 15 percent of all parents have used the V-chip; (2) 26 percent of all parents have not bought a new television set since January 2000 (when the V-chip was first required in *all* sets); (3) 39 percent of parents have bought a new television set since January 2000, but do not think it includes a V-chip; and (4) 20 percent of parents know they have a V-chip, but have not used it. According to a 2003 study, parents' low level of V-chip use is explained in part by parents' unawareness of the device and the "multi-step and often confusing process" necessary to use it. Only 27 percent of parents in the study group could figure out how to program the V-chip, and many parents "who might otherwise have used the V-chip were frustrated by an inability to get it to work properly." A March 2007 Zogby poll indicates, among other things, that 88 percent of respondents did not use a V-chip or cable box parental controls in the previous week, leading the Parents Television Council to call the television industry's V-chip education campaign "a failure."

In addition to mandating inclusion of V-chip technology in television sets, the Act provides cable subscribers with some ways to block unwanted programming. These provisions of the Act, however, do not benefit households receiving their television programming via over-the-air broadcasting or satellite. Further, similar to the V-chip, to take advantage of these measures a cable subscriber first must be aware of and then affirmatively request that such measures be employed. Finally, to receive these protections, a cable subscriber must take several steps and incur some costs. . . .

We believe that further action to enable viewer-initiated blocking of violent television content would serve the government's interests in protecting the well-being of children and facilitating parental supervision and would be reasonably likely to be upheld as constitutional. As indicated above, however, reliance on blocking technology alone would probably not fulfill the government's interest in protecting the well-being of children. Blocking technology does not ensure that children are prevented from viewing violent programming unless it is activated, and courts have recognized the practical limits of parental supervision.

Rating Systems

In addition, any successful viewer-initiated blocking regime with respect to violent programming would depend upon the adoption and successful implementation of an effective ratings system. Currently, to facilitate operation of the V-chip and other blocking mechanisms, broadcast, cable, and satellite television providers, on a voluntary basis, rate programming using the industry-devised TV ratings system guidelines and encode programs accordingly. Most television programming, except for news and sports programming, carries an age-based TV rating set by program networks and producers, and most include content-based ratings as well.

Studies and surveys demonstrate, however, that the voluntary TV ratings system is of limited effectiveness in protecting children from violent television content. In the 2004 Kaiser survey discussed above, 50 percent of all parents surveyed stated that they have used the TV ratings. But about 4 in 10 parents (39 percent) stated that most programs are not rated accurately, and many parents did not fully understand what the various ratings categories mean. For example, only 24 percent of parents of young children (two–six years old) could name any of the ratings that would apply to programming appropriate for children that age. Only 12 percent of parents knew that the rating FV ("fantasy violence") is related to violent content, while 8 percent thought it meant "family viewing." One in five (20 percent) parents said that they had never heard of the TV ratings system, an increase from 14 percent in 2000 and 2001. A more recent survey indicates that only 8 percent of respondents could correctly identify the categories.

And, of course, ratings can only be effective in protecting children from inappropriate content if the parent understands the ratings information, and such information is accurate. In a study published in the journal *Pediatrics*, parents concluded that half of television shows the industry had rated as appropriate for teenagers were in fact inappropriate, a finding the study authors called "a signal that the ratings are misleading." Academics who have studied the television rating system share parents' assessment that the ratings are often inaccurate. A 2002 study found that many shows that should carry content descriptors do not, therefore leaving parents unaware of potentially objectionable material. For example, the study found that 68 percent of prime-time network shows without an "L" descriptor contained "adult language," averaging nearly three scenes with such language per show. In fact, "in all four areas of sensitive material—violence, sexual behavior, sexual dialogue, and adult language—the large majority of programs that contain such depictions are not identi-fied by a content descriptor." The study's authors concluded that "[p]arents who might rely solely on the content-based catego-ries to block their children's exposure to objectionable portray-als would be making a serious miscalculation, as the content descriptors actually identify only a small minority of the full range of violence, sex, and adult language found on television." A 2004 study also raised serious questions about the accuracy of television ratings. It found that there was more coarse language broadcast during TV-PG programs than those rated TV-14, just the opposite of what these age-based ratings would lead a viewer to believe. The Parents Television Council ("PTC") and the Annenberg Public Policy Center also have conducted studies indicating that the voluntary TV ratings system is inaccurate, in-consistently applied, and cannot fully address parental concerns over children's TV viewing.

An economist studying the question of why networks con-sistently "underlabel" their programs concluded that they are likely responding to economic incentives. He found that pro-grams with more restrictive ratings command lower advertising revenues. The desire to charge more for commercials and fear of "advertiser backlash" over shows with more restrictive ratings "means that networks have incentives to resist the provision of content-based information."

To address these issues, Congress could seek to establish a mandatory ratings system that would address the shortcomings of the current system set forth above. Such a system could be defended on the grounds that it merely requires the disclosure of truthful information about a potentially harmful product (violent television programming), thereby advancing the compelling government interests without significantly burdening First Amendment rights. It could also be defended as a necessary predicate for the operation of a successful system of viewer-initiated blocking. As stated above, however, although mandatory television ratings would impose lesser burdens on protected speech, we believe the evidence demonstrates that they would not fully serve the government's interest in the well-being of minors given the limits of parental supervision recognized by the D.C. Circuit in *ACT III*. Experience also leads us to question whether such a ratings system would ever be sufficiently accurate given the myriad of practical difficulties that would accompany any comprehensive effort to ensure the accuracy of ratings. Moreover, such a requirement may have an unintended practical consequence. There is some evidence that TV ratings may actually serve to attract certain underage viewers to programming that is violent or is otherwise labeled as not intended for a child audience. . . .

In sum, Congress could implement a time channeling solution, as discussed above, and/or mandate some other form of consumer choice in obtaining video programming.

> "The FCC seems to think that parents are completely incompetent and that only benevolent-minded bureaucrats can save the day from objectionable fare that enters the home."

Parents, Not Government, Should Regulate Television Violence

Adam Thierer

In the following viewpoint, researcher Adam Thierer contends that the government's definition of violent programming is inadequate and ambiguous. He says people have different values, and parents are best positioned to impart their values to their children. He concludes that individual parental regulation is preferable to regulation by government bureaucrats. Thierer is a senior research fellow at the Mercatus Center at George Mason University.

As you read, consider the following questions:

1. According to Thierer, what is the problem with the Federal Communication Commission's recommendation to use judicial precedent to determine the definition of excessively violent programming?

2. What does Thierer say are the three categories of house-hold media consumption rules?

3. What does Thierer ask himself when he sees the Parents Television Council motto "Because Our Children Are Watching?"

The FCC [Federal Communications Commission] has just is-sued its long-awaited report on *Violent Television Program-ming and Its Impact on Children*. Unsurprisingly, it recommends that the government should assume a great role in regulating the video content that comes into our homes. The agency concludes that: "We believe that further action to enable viewer-initiated blocking of violent television content would serve the govern-ment's interests in protecting the well-being of children and facili-tating parental supervision and would be reasonably likely to be upheld as constitutional."

Ambiguous Language

Ironically, however, the FCC's report goes on to undercut its own argument for regulation again and again because of the stunning level of ambiguity surrounding everything they propose. For ex-ample, in the second paragraph of the report, the FCC notes that "A broad range of television programming aired today contains [violent] content, including, for example, cartoons, dramatic se-ries, professional sports such boxing, news coverage, and nature programs." Is the agency saying such things could be regulated? They never tell us.

Or consider the endless number of questions raised by this paragraph on pages 20–21:

We believe that developing an appropriate definition of ex-cessively violent programming would be possible, but such language needs to be narrowly tailored and in conformance with judicial precedent. Any definition would need to be clear enough to provide fair warning of the conduct required. A definition sufficient to give notice of upcoming violent programming content to parents and potential viewers could make use of, or be a refinement of, existing voluntary rating system definitions or could make use of definitions used in the research community when studying the consequences of violent programming. For more restrictive time channeling rules, a definition based on the scientific literature discussed above, which recognizes the factors most important to determining the likely impact of violence on the child audience, could be developed. For example, such a definition might cover depictions of physical force against an animate being that, in context, are patently offensive. In determining whether such depictions are patently offensive, the Government could consider among other factors the presence of weapons, whether the violence is extensive or graphic, and whether the violence is realistic.

Let's try to unpack some of this because defining "excessive violence" is really the core of this debate.

When the agency says "an appropriate definition of excessively violent programming . . . needs to be narrowly tailored and in conformance with judicial precedent," does the agency not realize that there is no such judicial precedent to look to here because what the FCC is proposing here is completely unprecedented?

When the agency says "a definition based on the scientific literature . . . which recognizes the factors most important to determining the likely impact of violence on the child audience" are they suggesting that a team of child psychologists should sign off on what programming is allowed or forbidden?

And does the agency really clarify things any when it says: "such a definition might cover depictions of physical force against an animate being that, in context, are patently offensive. In determining whether such depictions are patently offensive, the Government could consider among other factors the presence of weapons, whether the violence is extensive or graphic, and whether the violence is realistic." Needless to say, "depictions of physical force against an animate being that . . . are patently offensive" is a fairly open-ended regulatory mandate.

And saying that "patently offensive" programming might be defined so as to include "the presence of weapons, whether the violence is extensive or graphic, and whether the violence is realistic" doesn't really help us all that much. Would *Saving Private Ryan* [a 1998 film about World War II] or *Schindler's List* [a 1993 film about the Holocaust] be regulated under that standard? Where would news reports or documentaries about wars fall under that standard?

And when the agency talks about "whether the violence is realistic" as part of the standard, which way do they mean? If the violence is more realistic, is that good or bad? I ask that question because I sometimes hear some media critics bemoaning the fact that fantasy or animated violence doesn't portray the actual consequences of violence.

We get no answers to any of these questions. The ambiguity in this report is so thick that you could cut it with a knife. (Wait, bad analogy. The FCC might fine me for that!)

But don't take my word about the ambiguous, open-ended nature of this report or the Pandora's Box of regulatory shenanigans that the FCC is opening up here. Listen to what FCC Commissioner Jonathan Adelstein had to say about the report in his statement today:

> The Commission has not been able to formulate and recommend a definition of violence that would cover the majority of violent content that is inappropriate for children, provide fair guidance to programmers, and stand a decent chance of withstanding constitutional scrutiny, in light of judicial precedent. While we may want to define prohibited-violence and regulate it in conformance with constitutional standards, the *Report*

does not refer to any court or judicial scholar that has suggested such definition is available or probable. To the contrary, the *Report* diminishes the extent to which courts have either expressed serious skepticism or invalidated efforts to regulate violent content. . . .

Are Parents Incompetent?

But let's just set aside all those meddlesome First Amendment matters for a moment and talk about some [of] the other flawed assumptions upon which the agency's report is built.

Reading through this report, one is struck by the fact that the FCC seems to think that parents are completely incompetent and that only benevolent-minded bureaucrats can save the day from objectionable fare that enters the home. The agency repeats the criticisms leveled by media critics and regulatory activists like the Parents Television Council and Morality in Media who claim that technical controls (ratings, V-Chip, cable set-top box controls, etc) have been a failure. The report concludes that: "although the V-chip and TV ratings system appear useful in the abstract, they are not effective at protecting children from violent content" . . . and "it does not appear that cable operator-provided advanced parental controls are available on a sufficient number of cable-connected television sets to be considered an effective solution at this time."

Ironically, the FCC can't even figure out what it really wants to say on this front. Consider this rather remarkable paragraph:

> Experience also leads us to question whether such a ratings system would ever be sufficiently accurate given the myriad of practical difficulties that would accompany any comprehensive effort to ensure the accuracy of ratings. Moreover, such a requirement may have an unintended practical consequence. There is some evidence that TV ratings may actually serve to attract certain underage viewers to programming that is violent or is otherwise labeled as not intended for a child audience.

What a peculiar argument. On the one hand, the FCC tells us that the current TV ratings don't work because they don't provide parents enough information. But here, on the other hand, they're saying that if the ratings system worked perfectly and described violent content accurately then the old "forbidden fruit" problem would kick in and kids would just try harder to watch such programming. Basically, there's just no winning with the agency; they seem determined to find a justification for regulating using any rationale possible.

But what of the argument that the current ratings and blocking tools are ineffective? It's rubbish. Either the FCC and the critics have never bothered trying to use the tools or they are nit-picking with the definitions of certain types of content that they feel was offensive and not blocked by a certain rating. That's the problem with arguments like those made by the Parents Television Council [PTC] and other regulatory advocates. In an attempt to persuade regulators to reshape television through regulation in the way they desire, these critics claim that certain words or images should have been screened according to their standards. Is "bitch" an indecent word? The PTC thinks so. But many in the public use it every day. So when a TV programmer doesn't tighten a show's rating because that word is uttered, is that really a failure of the ratings system? Same goes for violence. A pillow fight on *The Brady Bunch* would probably lead to calls for an "TV-MA [Mature Audiences Only]" rating from some of these groups.

What critics consistently forget—or perhaps intentionally ignore—is that media ratings and content labeling efforts are not an exact science; they are fundamentally subjective exercises. Ratings are based on value judgments made by humans who all have somewhat different values. Those doing the rating are being asked to evaluate artistic expression and assign labels to it that provide the rest of us with some rough proxies about what is in that particular piece of art, or what age group should (or should not) be consuming it. Thus, the critics can always claim there are "flaws" in a ratings systems but that's only because humans all have different perspectives and values that they will use to label or classify content. But that doesn't mean the ratings can't be an effective tool that can help parents screen out a great deal of material they might find undesirable.

Household Rules

But let's forget about ratings and technical controls like the V-Chip and set-top boxes for a moment. Why? Because many parents forget about them. That is, many parents just ignore technical controls altogether and opt for informal household media rules instead. In fact, a 2003 Kaiser Family Foundation survey found that "Almost all parents say they have some type of rules about their children's use of media." And a 2006 Kaiser survey of families with infants and preschoolers revealed that 85 percent of those parents who let their children watch TV at that age have rules about what their child can and cannot watch. 63 percent of those parents say they enforce those rules all of the time. (Incidentally, about the same percentage of parents said they had similar rules for video game and computer usage.)

Parents employ a wide variety of household media consumption rules. Some of these can be quite formal in the sense that parents make the rules clear and enforce them routinely in the home over a long period of time. Other media consumption rules can be fairly informal, however, and be enforced on a more selective basis. Regardless, these household media consumption rules can be grouped into three general categories: (1) "Where" rules; (2) "When and how much" rules; and, (3) "Under what conditions" rules.

For example, many families establish "where" rules regarding the placement of TVs or other media devices in the home. In our home, my wife and I have assigned our kids a specific TV for the limited selection of programming we allow them [to] watch and that TV is located in the living room where we keep an eye or ear

Parents Must Take Responsibility

We, parents, must take responsibility for the media that is viewed *inside* our homes, but also must be active in changing the media landscape *outside* our homes. I encourage all parents to let your local TV station know when something you find inappropriate is aired, and be sure to notify your representatives in Congress. If enough parents speak out, perhaps we will not only improve the tools that are available to parents to help minimize their children's exposure to violent content, but we will actually see an increase in the amount of family-friendly, uplifting and nonviolent programming being produced.

Deborah Taylor Tate, "Statement," in
Federal Communications Commission, In the
Matter of Violent Television Programming
and Its Impact on Children, *FCC 07-56,*
April 6, 2007. http://hraunfoss.fcc.gov.

on what the kids are watching at all times. And all of us probably heard this "under what condition" rule at some point in our childhood: "You have to finish your homework before you get to watch any TV." And an example of a "when and how much" rule would be: "No TV or video games after 8:00," or, more stringently: "No TV or games on a school night."

Many families get even more creative by devising a "media allowance" for their children (especially as they get older) to allow them to consume media within certain boundaries. In our home, my wife and I generally allow our kids one hour of TV viewing per night on weeknights, and two hours on Saturdays and Sundays. Carrot-and-stick incentives can also be used with this approach. For example, better behavior or improved grades at school might be rewarded by adding additional viewing time to their overall weekly media allowance.

Of course, there's a fourth category that could be added to the list of informal household media rules listed above: "what" rules. As in, what we allow our kids to watch at all. According to The Pew Internet & American Life Project, 77 percent of parents already have rules for what TV shows their kids can watch, 67 percent have rules for what kind of video games they can play, and 85 percent have rules about what Internet websites they can and cannot visit. . . .

Such informal household media rules are a vitally important, yet frequently overlooked, part of this debate. In fact, the FCC never even bothers mentioning such things in its new report. Certainly a few of the good folks down at the FCC are parents themselves. Do they not have such household media rules at work in their homes? I bet they do. And I bet a significant percentage of them just ignore all the other technologies altogether and opt exclusively for such informal household rules like many other American households.

But if you're focused on adding fuel to the flames of an already burning political crusade, then I suppose you wouldn't want to mention things like this. The FCC just asks us to believe that parents are completely helpless against these supposed technological "invaders" into our homes. You know . . . those damn $2,000 televisions that magically walked into our homes, and those meddlesome $50-a-month cable and satellite boxes and subscriptions. How dare those devices come into our homes uninvited and make us watch them! Please FCC . . . save us from ourselves! . . .

Personal Responsibility

The Parents Television Council, which seems to have the ear of FCC officials on this and other content regulation issues, has an interesting motto: "Because Our Children Are Watching." It's a tagline they use all over their website and in all their printed materials. Presumably it means that they believe regulation is justified because our children are watching television in our homes.

But whenever I see that "Because Our Children Are Watching" tagline I always ask myself: Why? Why are your children watching? Why are you letting your children watch shows you might find offensive or harmful? Do you not exercise any control over your kids? Do they run the household, or do you? Weren't you the one to bring those TVs, cable boxes and satellite dishes home? Did you not set up any ground rules about what they can watch once you brought those things into the home? Do you not limit their viewing time? Do you not turn the TV off and make them do other things? Do you not talk to them about what's on TV, what you find inappropriate, and what the difference is between fantasy and reality?

Honestly, I just don't get it. Why do critics like the PTC and their many allies in this fight give lip service to the notion that parents should be the "first line of defense" in terms of the video programming that enters the home, but then they turn around and vociferously advocate that five unelected bureaucrats at the FCC step in as a surrogate parent for our children? Let us be clear on this point: If you advocate a role for the government in terms of regulating violent programming on television then you have made those regulators the primary party in charge of what comes into the home. When government regulates speech it acts on everyone's behalf and tells us what it thinks is best for *all of us* and *all families*.

That's not how things should work in a free society. Decisions about acceptable media content are extraordinarily personal; no two people or families will have the same set of values, especially in a nation as diverse as ours. Consequently, it would be optimal if public policy decisions in this field took into account the extraordinary diversity of citizen/household tastes and left the ultimate decision about acceptable content to them. That's especially the case in light of the fact that most U.S. households are made up entirely of adults. According to the Census Bureau, only one-third of U.S. households include children under the age of 18.

Whatever happened to personal and parental responsibility in this country? I'm looking out for my own kids. FCC officials and the media critics should look out for theirs and quit treating the rest of us like we're all children.

> "California's marginal control on the sale or rental of violent video games to minors is within the permissible advancement of a significant . . . public interest in protecting the development and mental health of minors."

Violent Video Games Cause Aggression in Children and Should Be Regulated

Steven F. Gruel

In the following viewpoint, attorney Steven F. Gruel maintains that scientific evidence shows video games are harmful to children. He argues that in the United States, the First Amendment to the US Constitution, which guarantees freedom of speech, has legally been limited in cases involving harm to children. He concludes that the state of California has the legal right to regulate the sale of violent video games to children. Gruel is a criminal defense attorney in San Francisco.

As you read, consider the following questions:

1. According to Gruel, what sort of content is included in M-rated video games?

Steven F. Gruel, Brief of Amicus Curiae, *Schwarzenegger v. Video Software Dealers Association and Entertainment Software Association*, July 19, 2010. Supreme Court of The United States.

2. What effect does Gruel say video games can have on the frontal cortex of the brain?

3. Why does children's autonomy deserve less respect from the state than the autonomy of adults, according to Gruel?

California Civil Code Sections 1746–1746.5 prohibit the sale of violent video games to minors under 18 where a reasonable person would find that the violent content appeals to a deviant or morbid interest of minors, is patently offensive to prevailing community standards as to what is suitable for minors, and causes the games as [a] whole to lack serious literary, artistic, political, or scientific value for minors. The respondent industry groups challenged this prohibition on its face as violating the Free Speech Clause of the First Amendment. The court of appeals affirmed the district court's judgment permanently enjoining enforcement of the prohibition.

The questions presented are:

1. Does the First Amendment bar a state from restricting the sale and rental of violent video games to minors?

2. If the First Amendment applies to violent video games that are sold to minors, and the standard of review is strict scrutiny, under *Turner Broadcasting System, Inc. v. F.C.C.*, 512 U.S. 622, 666 (1994), is the state required to demonstrate a direct causal link between violent video games and physical and psychological harm to minors before the state can prohibit the sale of the games to minors?

Protecting Minors

By any measure, California has a compelling interest in protecting the physical and psychological care of minors. When juxtaposed against the backdrop of protecting the First Amendment, this [the Supreme] Court has held that the Constitution does not confer the protection on communication aimed at children as it does for adults. When weighing the conflicting concerns of minors this Court correctly carved a flexible standard of review and not a strict scrutiny approach. We know, of course, that a state can prohibit the sale of sexually-explicit material to minors under a "variable obscenity" or "obscenity as to minors" standard. *Ginsberg v. New York*, 390 U.S. 629 (1968). Just as it was rational for the State to conclude that that type of material was harmful to minors, the restrictions to assist parents in protecting their children's well-being is, in a practical sense, no different than the concerns supporting California's enactment of California Civil Code Sections 1746–1746.5.

Indeed, restricting the sale and rental of extremely violent interactive videos to minors advances the very same societal interests understood in *Ginsberg*. Contrary to the Ninth Circuit's perception, *Ginsberg* was not meant to exclusively apply to sexually explicit materials, but can and should apply to equally harmful materials depicting violence.

Needless to say, the world is much different today than it was in 1968 when *Ginsberg* was decided. What *has* remained for the past 40 years, however, is the commonsense understanding that the First Amendment does not protect materials harmful to minors.

Immersion and Video Games

In 2006, a Federal Trade Commission study revealed that nearly 70 percent of 13 to 16 year olds are able to successfully purchase Mature or M-rated video games. These M-rated games, labeled by the industry as such in an attempt to voluntarily "police" the distribution of harmful videos, are designed specifically for adults. The content in these types of games enable the user to murder, burn, and maim law enforcement officers, racial minorities, and members of clergy as well as sexually assault women.

In his March 29, 2006 testimony submitted to the Subcommittee on the Constitution, Civil Rights, and Property Rights of the United States Senate Judiciary Committee, [state] Senator

[Leland] Yee noted that the interactive nature of video games is vastly different than passively listening to music, watching a movie, or reading a book. With interactive video games, the child becomes a part of the action which serves as a potent agent to facilitate violence, and over time learns the destructive behavior. This immersion results in a more powerful experience and potentially dangerous learned behavior in children and youth. In fact, often times it is the same technology that our military and police use to simulate and train for real life battle conditions and violent law enforcement confrontations in the community.

Moreover, there is a practical side in favor of the State's effort to regulate the sale or rental of violent video games to children. Parents can read a book, watch a movie or listen to a CD to discern if it is appropriate for their child. These violent video games, on the other hand, can contain up to 800 hours of footage with the most atrocious content often reserved for the highest levels that can be accessed only by advanced players after hours upon hours of progressive mastery.

Just as the technology of video games improves at astonishing rates, so too does the body of research consistently demonstrate the harmful effects these violent interactive games have on minors. Hundreds of peer-reviewed studies, produced over a period of 30 years documenting the effects of screen violence (including violent video games), have now been published in the professional journals of the American Academy of Pediatrics, American Academy of Child and Adolescent Psychiatry, American Psychological Association, American Medical Association, American Academy of Family Physicians, and the American Psychiatric Association and others. . . .

Heightened Aggression

Some of the most recent research addressing this serious concern [includes] meta-analysis of approximately 130 studies pertaining to the effects of playing violent video games which was published in March 2010.

These data continually and strongly suggest that participating in the playing of violent video games by children increases aggressive thought and behavior; increases antisocial behavior and delinquency; engenders poor school performance; and desensitizes the game player to violence.

Notably, extended play has been observed to depress activity in the frontal cortex of the brain which controls executive thought and function, produces intentionality and the ability to plan sequences of action, and is the seat of self-reflection, discipline and self-control.

Also, United States Surgeon General David Satcher warned in his *Report on Youth Violence* (2000) of a demonstrated link between screen violence and subsequent physical aggression in children and adolescents that is stronger than the link between secondhand smoke and cancer.

Finally, new data shows that the intensity of interactive video games may be habituating and that 2 to 3 hour sessions of intense interactions with video games raise adrenaline levels in children and produces extended physiological arousal. In the medical community concern has been raised at prolonged and regularly repeated states of adrenalized arousal and hyper-vigilance involved in children watching violent video games and the possible harmful effects on still developing bodies and brains.

These studies demonstrate that playing ultraviolent games can cause automatic aggressiveness, increase aggressive thoughts and behavior, antisocial behavior, desensitization, poor school performance and reduced activity in the frontal lobes of the brain.

Society Has an Interest in Protecting Minors

As a society, we understand the clear unequivocal commonsense reasons to prohibit the sale of alcohol, tobacco, firearms, driver's licenses and pornography to minors. That same reasoning applies in the foundation and enactment of California Civil Code

Sections 1746–1746.5. Given that the First Amendment does not protect the State's restriction on the sale or rental of harmful violent video games to minors, the Court should reverse the decision of the Ninth Circuit Court of Appeals and uphold the California law as a statutory safeguard necessary in this modern day world.

This Court has long agreed that there is an overriding justification in protecting children from conduct pervasive in society. Without question, restricting a minor's access to gambling, smoking and alcohol serve the community's interest in both protecting a minor's development as well as safeguarding against the individual and widespread collateral consequences which flow from a minor's early addiction to these vices.

As a general proposition, many constitutional rights vary in the degree to which the exercise of the right by minors is protected from government abridgment. For example, minors do not have the right to exercise the franchise. Similarly, a minor's right to have an abortion may be subject to regulations that would be rejected as unduly burdensome if they were applied to adult women. Thus, there is a recognized foundation for distinguishing between minors and adults in analyzing the constitutionality of regulations.

This foundation comports with the common sense intuition that, because children lack maturity to make wise judgments, their autonomy deserves less respect from the state than does the autonomy of adults. While paternalistic state regulations are correctly viewed as demeaning when applied to adults, they are considered appropriate, if not necessary, for children.

In *Ginsberg*, of course, this Court concluded that the State had greater authority to limit the exercise of protected freedoms because children were involved and, in relying on its precedents, recognized that "the State has an interest 'to protect the welfare of children' and to see that they are 'safeguarded from abuses' which might prevent 'their growth into free and independent well-developed men and citizens.'"

As it relates to expressive materials, there is no language from this Court suggesting that the State's interest in protecting minors from such material *is limited* to speech with sexual content. In *Erznoznik v. City of Jacksonville*, a case concerning restrictions on films depicting nudity from being shown in drive-in movies, the Court was unwilling to protect minors from brief exposure to such images.

However, the alleged harm caused by the minimal exposure to nude images a child passing by a drive-in theater might witness cannot realistically be compared to harm resulting from repeated and long term exposure to violent video games. In fact, in *FCC v. Pacifica Foundation*, 438 U.S. 726 (1978), this Court supported an FCC [Federal Communications Commission] determination that the radio broadcast of a George Carlin monologue containing "filthy words" could be restricted precisely because it was accessible to young children.

Children Are Different

Children, this Court has acknowledged, are different in the eyes of the law because of brain development. *Ropers v. Simmons*, 543 U.S. 551 (2005). Under the "evolving standards of decency" test, the *Ropers* Court held that it was cruel and unusual punishment to execute a person who was under the age of 18 at the time of the murder. Writing for the majority, Justice [Anthony] Kennedy cited a body of sociological and scientific research that found that juveniles have a lack of maturity and sense of responsibility compared to adults. Adolescents were found to be over-represented statistically in virtually every category of reckless behavior.

In *Ropers*, the Court noted that in recognition of the comparative immaturity and irresponsibility of juveniles, almost every state prohibited those under age 18 from voting, serving on juries, or marrying without parental consent. The studies also found that juveniles are also more vulnerable to negative influences and outside pressures, including peer pressure. They have less control, or experience with control, over their own environment. More recently, in *Graham v. Florida*, 130 S.Ct. 2011 (2010) this Court used the same rationale in finding that some life sentences without parole for minors were unconstitutional. This unequivocal commonsense approach by the Court to constitutional matters and children should be likewise applied in addressing the deepening dangers to minors from violent video games.

In sum, "[A] state or municipality can adopt more stringent controls on communicative materials available to youths than on those available to adults." [As stated in the] *Erznoznik* [court decision].

Here, California's marginal control on the sale or rental of violent video games to minors is within the permissible advancement of a significant, if not compelling, public interest in protecting the development and mental health of minors.

California's concern for its minors in the modern violent video game world is not fanciful or without basis. Science supports the legislative public policy determination.

> "A California law [had] said it shall be
> illegal to sell, rent, describe, admit the
> existence of, or otherwise disseminate
> a violent video game to minors, even
> if they can join the Army after their
> birthday tomorrow and get a serious
> gun with actual bullets."

Regulating Violent Video Games Is Unnecessary

James Lileks

James Lileks is a writer and the creator of the design and commentary website lileks.com. In June 2011 the US Supreme Court struck down a California law that made it illegal to distribute violent video games to younger audiences. In the following viewpoint Lileks argues that the Supreme Court should take on "real issues" such as freedom of speech. He believes that even if the court had upheld the law banning the selling of certain violent games to a minor, there is nothing to stop that child from borrowing the game from a friend. Furthermore, violence is not restricted to realistic video games and can be found in every aspect of society, including in classics of literature and other art forms.

As you read, consider the following questions:

1. According to the article, the US Supreme Court notes that violence abounds where else aside from video games?
2. How has the press described the videogame Grand Theft Auto?
3. As stated in the viewpoint, what is a good resource for parents to discover what a video game is about?

While the dead-eyed child squirms in your hands, piteously begging to be freed, the voice in your head gives you a choice: kill it, or save it. You suspect there will be consequences either way.

That's a scenario in the video game BioShock, and you can imagine the outrage: This is entertainment? What sort of culture produces such depravity? Perhaps this will help: The child is possessed by a drug-induced insanity, she's accompanied by a lumbering robot that wants to kill you, you're in a ruined underwater city populated by people driven mad by genetic manipulation, and the entire story is about a society constructed along the principles of [Russian-American novelist and philosopher] Ayn Rand.

Hope that helps. If not, play the game. BioShock rewards your humanity, plays with your loyalties, picks apart your character's sanity. It's a way of telling a story that some hesitate to call Art, because unlike [in the celebrated literature by Russian author Leo] Tolstoy, you can shoot fireballs from your hand. But for the kids who grew up controlling digital alter egos, it's high literature—and was probably illegal for minors in California. Until the courts weighed in.

The Courts

Late in June the Supremes [i.e., US Supreme Court justices] struck down a California law that said it shall be illegal to sell, rent, describe, admit the existence of, or otherwise disseminate a violent video game to minors, even if they can join the Army after their birthday tomorrow [i.e., after turning eighteen] and get a serious gun with actual bullets. The decision contained lots of solid eye-glazing constitutional folderol, most of which confounds parents who wonder why it shouldn't be illegal to sell a ten-year-old StrangleFest Death Party. (But Mom! The controller vibrates to simulate the death throes of your victims! Timmy has it! Pleeeeeze!) Shouldn't the Supreme Court take on real issues, like whether protected speech includes marching right down to the store that sold your kid the horrible game and giving them a piece of your mind?

Some on the right liked the pushback of a speech-regulating law; others worried about the kinder-kulture coarseness of shoot-'em-ups. Either way, you can't say it was a glib decision: The Court noted that literature abounds with violence, citing some torture-porn from [ancient Greek poet] Homer. This might be relevant if kids were playing Homer simulators. But reading is not doing; watching is not doing. Games are kinetic entertainment activities, if you will. They're spellbinding and immersive. There will always be those who see such statutes in the continuum of hapless prudery: Why, back in the 19th century, there were laws preventing an adult from describing a bout of fisticuffs with semaphore flags if there was a minor present. That comstockery was struck down by the courts, too. Same thing here. But not really.

Realism in Video Games

Today's games contain much more realistic depictions of ballistic perforations. "Realism," however, is a shifting standard. In the mid-1990s, which is two geological ages ago in gamer terms, there was "controversy" over [video game] Doom, which now looks like you're fighting off angry pieces of Lego. Duke Nukem [a video game] provided a ration of hysteria when someone heard from someone else that the player could shoot strippers. Ink was spilled like blood in the last reel of a [Sam] Peckinpah

"They say they're speaking out against violent video games."

film, condemning this new low, but it missed the point. You could shoot anything in the game. If, however, you hit what we call in the post-Weiner[1] era a "featured dancer," you would be swarmed by policemen who had been mutated into bipedal hogs by space aliens, and you would die. It was the game's way of establishing a moral code.

Yes, that sounds silly. You like to think that all your parenting instilled the "don't shoot the strippers" lesson early on, if only by the behavior you modeled. But then a gamer of a certain age hears about games like Grand Theft Auto, which most disapproving press accounts describe as a sociopathic instruction kit on the best way to apply a tire iron to a streetwalker, and the gamer yearns for the old days when there were codes of honor.

Oh, for the simple Manichean duality of [1970s video game] Pong! Then Pac-Man [a 1980s video game] ruined everything by making us seek the fruit at the expense of our own safety. That's when it all fell apart.

If games weren't the primary daily entertainment option for millions of minor boys, it might not be an issue. But concern over a few bad games vilifies titles like L.A. Noire—you're a cop in a [detective fiction writer Raymond] Chandler world—or the sprawling western [game] Red Dead Redemption. Not for the [Winnie the] Pooh set, but if they're off-limits to a 16-year-old, then so's a Road Runner cartoon.

Basic kvetch: Does there have to be a law, for heaven's sake? When you have a law that says kids can't buy the game, but shall borrow a friend's copy on the sly, then you get rulings that establish a minor's free-speech right to Grand Theft Auto, which means you'll have a kid sue his parents because they didn't give him Chainsaw Bob Orphanage Fracas IV for Christmas. It's not hard for parents to find out what a game's about, thanks to this thing called "the Internet." They might be alarmed to learn there's also a popular game in which small children are encouraged to imprison creatures in cramped, dark spheres, letting them out only to battle in cockfights that often send one to the hospital. [Pro football player] Michael Vick got put away for something like that.

The game goes by the name of Pokemon.

By the way, if you release the child in BioShock, you get all sorts of rewards. Never met a gamer who didn't let the kid go.

Note

1. The author is referring to Anthony Weiner, a congressman from the State of New York, who resigned in 2011 following a sex scandal.

> "The PG rating indicates, in the view of the Rating Board, that parents may consider some material unsuitable for their children, and parents should make that decision."

Movie Ratings Help Flag Violent Content That Is Inappropriate for Children

Motion Picture Association of America

The Motion Picture Association of America (MPAA) is a membership organization of the major US motion picture studios. It administers the film industry's voluntary ratings system. In the following viewpoint, the MPAA explains the ratings system, which acts as a guide to parents as to which films are appropriate for children. The system runs from G films, which are deemed appropriate for all audiences, through NC-17 films, to which children under seventeen will not be admitted.

As you read, consider the following questions:

1. According to the MPAA, what things are not permitted in a G-rated film?

2. Under what circumstances does the MPAA say that a movie may receive a PG-13 rating even if it includes an expletive used in a sexual context?
3. Does an NC-17 rating imply a negative judgment on a film, according to the MPAA? Explain your answer.

Editor's note: The following descriptions explain the meaning of the MPAA ratings.

G—*General Audiences. All ages admitted.* A G-rated motion picture contains nothing in theme, language, nudity, sex, violence or other matters that, in the view of the Rating Board, would offend parents whose younger children view the motion picture. The G rating is not a "certificate of approval" nor does it signify a "children's" motion picture. Some snippets of language may go beyond polite conversation but they are common everyday expressions. No stronger words are present in G-rated motion pictures. Depictions of violence are minimal. No nudity, sex scenes or drug use are present in the motion picture.

PG—Parental Guidance Suggested. Some material may not be suitable for children. A PG-rated motion picture should be investigated by parents before they let their younger children attend. The PG rating indicates, in the view of the Rating Board, that parents may consider some material unsuitable for their children, and parents should make that decision. The more mature themes in some PG-rated motion pictures may call for parental guidance. There may be some profanity and some depictions of violence or brief nudity. But these elements are not deemed so intense as to require that parents be strongly cautioned beyond the suggestion of parental guidance. There is no drug use content in a PG-rated motion picture.

Increasingly Mature Content

PG-13—Parents Strongly Cautioned. Some material may be inappropriate for children under 13. A PG-13 rating is a sterner warning by the Rating Board to parents to determine whether their children under age 13 should view the motion picture, as some material might not be suited for them. A PG-13 motion picture may go beyond the PG rating in theme, violence, nudity, sensuality, language, adult activities or other elements, but does not reach the restricted R category. The theme of the motion picture by itself will not result in a rating greater than PG-13, although depictions of activities related to a mature theme may result in a restricted rating for the motion picture. Any drug use will initially require at least a PG-13 rating. More than brief nudity will require at least a PG-13 rating, but such nudity in a PG-13 rated motion picture generally will not be sexually oriented. There may be depictions of violence in a PG-13 movie, but generally not both realistic and extreme or persistent violence. A motion picture's single use of one of the harsher sexually-derived words, though only as an expletive, initially requires at least a PG-13 rating. More than one such expletive requires an R rating, as must even one of those words used in a sexual context. The Rating Board nevertheless may rate such a motion picture PG-13 if, based on a special vote by a two-thirds majority, the Raters feel that most American parents would believe that a PG-13 rating is appropriate because of the context or manner in which the words are used or because the use of those words in the motion picture is inconspicuous.

R—Restricted. Children under 17 require accompanying parent or adult guardian. R-rated motion picture, in the view of the Rating Board, contains some adult material. An R-rated motion picture may include adult themes, adult activity, hard language, intense or persistent violence, sexually-oriented nudity, drug abuse or other elements, so that parents are counseled to take this rating very seriously. Children under 17 are not allowed to attend R-rated motion pictures unaccompanied by a parent or adult guardian. Parents are strongly urged to find out more about R-rated motion pictures in determining their suitability for their children. Generally, it is not appropriate for parents to bring their young children with them to R-rated motion pictures.

NC-17—No One 17 and Under Admitted. An NC-17 rated motion picture is one that, in the view of the Rating Board, most parents would consider patently too adult for their children 17 and under. No children will be admitted. NC-17 does not mean "obscene" or "pornographic" in the common or legal meaning of those words, and should not be construed as a negative judgment in any sense. The rating simply signals that the content is appropriate only for an adult audience. An NC-17 rating can be based on violence, sex, aberrational behavior, drug abuse or any other element that most parents would consider too strong and therefore off-limits for viewing by their children.

> *"Currently, there are no movie industry standards for Internet advertising, and the report notes violent R-rated movies were routinely advertised on Web sites popular with kids."*

Despite Ratings, Children Are Still Exposed to Violent Media

Federal Trade Commission (FTC)

The Federal Trade Commission (FTC) is a US federal agency entrusted with consumer protection. In the following viewpoint, the FTC reports that the video game industry has made some progress in restricting the sale of violent content to children. However, the film, music, and video game industries all continue to market or advertise inappropriately violent content to children under seventeen. The FTC suggests that the industries take further steps to restrict and label marketing of violent content to children.

As you read, consider the following questions:

1. What guidelines for marketing inappropriate content have several individual movie studios adopted, according to the FTC?

"FTC Issues Report on Marketing Violent Entertainment to Children," Federal Trade Commission, April 12, 2007.

2. According to the FTC, what statistics indicate an overall positive picture of the game rating system in terms of parent awareness?

3. What problems with marketing violent content did the FTC find on video and social networking sites such as YouTube and MySpace?

The Federal Trade Commission [FTC] gave a mixed review of the movie, music, and video-game industries' self-regulatory programs and their marketing of violent entertainment products to children in its latest [2007] report to Congress. This fifth follow-up report, the most comprehensive study since 2000, found that all three industries generally comply with their own voluntary standards regarding the display of ratings and labels. However, entertainment industries continue to market some R-rated [Restricted] movies, M-rated [Mature] video games, and explicit-content recordings on television shows and Web sites with substantial teen audiences. In addition, the FTC found that while video game retailers have made significant progress in limiting sales of M-rated games to children, movie and music retailers have made only modest progress limiting sales.

Undercover Shopping Finds Improvements

"Self-regulation, long a critical underpinning of U.S. advertising, is weakened if industry markets products in ways inconsistent with their ratings and parental advisories," said FTC Chairman Deborah Platt Majoras. "This latest FTC report shows improvement, but also indicates that the entertainment industry has more work to do."

The report includes results from the FTC's latest mystery shop where unaccompanied children, ages 13–16, were sent into retailers to make a purchase. The undercover shop found significant improvement by video-game retailers, particularly in national retail chains, but little or no improvement by movie theaters, or DVD and music retailers.

Other findings in the report include:

Movies. Although there is no industry-wide standard, several individual movie studios have adopted guidelines restricting advertising on television shows where the under-17 audience is more than 35%. The study found a few examples of R-rated movies and unrated DVD advertisements on television shows where the under-17 audience exceeded 35%, but most television ads were placed on shows that fell under this threshold. Nevertheless, the report notes that a 35% standard still permits advertising on the vast majority of shows most popular with teens. Currently, there are no movie industry standards for Internet advertising, and the report notes violent R-rated movies were routinely advertised on Web sites popular with kids: 18 of the 20 movies studied by the Commission were advertised on Web sites where more than a third of the audience was under 17. The increasing prevalence of marketing unrated DVDs containing content that might warrant an NC-17 rating, coupled with the poor performance of retailers in restricting the sales of such DVDs to unaccompanied children, is a particular cause for concern.

Music. Because the music labeling system is not age-based, the industry has no specific restrictions on advertising explicit-content labeled music in media popular with children. The report notes that ads for explicit-content music routinely aired on cable television shows and Web sites with a teen audience of 40% or more. The industry also needs to do a better job of displaying the explicit-content logo in television advertising. On the plus side, the industry continues to refrain from significant advertising in magazines popular with teens, a practice that was prevalent when the Commission published its initial report in September 2000.

Percent of Children Able to Make the Purchase Unaccompanied

These data represent the results of the FTC's mystery shop where children, ages 13–16, were sent into retailers to make a purchase.

	2000	2001	2003	2006
R-Rated Movie Theater Ticket	46%	48%	36%*	39%
R-Rated Movie on DVD	N/A	N/A	81%	71%*
Unrated Movie on DVD	N/A	N/A	N/A	71%
Explicit-Content Labeled Music Recording	85%	90%	83%	76%*
M-Rated Electronic Game	85%	78%*	69%*	42%*

*Denotes a statistically significant change

TAKEN FROM: FTC, "FTC Issues Report on Marketing Violent Entertainment to Children," April 12, 2007. www.ftc.gov.

Video Games. Although ads for M-rated video games on television shows that are popular with teens appear to be diminishing, the same is not true for Internet advertising. Currently, the ESRB [Entertainment Software Review Board] prohibits ads for M-rated games on Web sites where the under-17 audience is 45% or more. The report suggests that the ESRB is not adequately enforcing even this limited standard. The video game industry generally provides clear and prominent disclosure of rating information in advertising; however, the ESRB has not adopted the Commission's previous recommendation that content descriptors for games be placed on the front of game packaging. The Commission's survey of parents and children on their awareness and use of the video game ratings system showed an overall positive picture of the game rating system: 87% of parents surveyed said they are aware of the ESRB system, more than seven in ten use it when their child wants to play a game for the first time, and three quarters of the parents who are familiar with the content descriptors use them. However, many parents still believe the system can do more to inform them about the level of violence in some games.

Better Oversight and Tighter Standards

For the first time, the Commission tracked trends in viral marketing, including social networking sites such as MySpace, and viral video sites like YouTube. Advertisers often set up profile pages with industry-generated content or uploaded videos for users to then share on their own, such as posting music to their own profile page or emailing videos to friends. The report noted that few profile pages contain prominent rating information. Although they are general audience sites, they reach a large number of children under 17. The report also flags a new trend in gaming, mobile phone games, and noted several challenges they pose. For example, mobile phone game developers often do not seek ESRB ratings and they do not sell their products through traditional retail channels, instead licensing their products directly to wireless carriers. The report discusses industry efforts to provide some form of parental oversight in this fledgling area.

The FTC recommends that all three industries consider adopting new, or tightening existing, target marketing standards. The FTC also suggests retailers further implement and enforce point-of-sale policies restricting sales of rated or labeled material to children under 17. In particular, the report suggests the movie industry examine whether marketing and selling of unrated or "Director's Cut" DVD versions of R-rated movies, which may contain content that could warrant an even more restrictive rating, undermines the current self-regulatory system. The report also suggests that the music industry provide more information on packaging and in advertising about why certain recordings receive a Parental Advisory. Finally, the report recommends that the video game industry place content descriptors on the front of product packaging and research why many parents believe that the system could do a better job of informing them about the level of violence in some games.

The Commission continues to support industry self-regulation in this area given important First Amendment considerations. The Commission will continue to monitor this area, particularly as emerging technologies change the way entertainment products are marketed and sold. The Commission also will continue to work with industry and others to encourage efforts to provide parents with the information they need to decide which products are appropriate for their children.

Periodical and Internet Sources Bibliography

The following articles have been selected to supplement the diverse views presented in this chapter.

Brad J. Bushman	"The Effects of Violent Video Games. Do They Affect Our Behavior?," *ITHP*, n.d., 2011. http://ithp.org.
Andy Chalk	"Australian Study 'Confirms Dangers of Violent Videogames,'" *The Escapist*, November 1, 2011. www.escapistmagazine.com.
Roger Ebert	"Getting Real About Movie Ratings," *Wall Street Journal*, December 11, 2010. http://online .wsj.com.
Brandon Fibbs	"MPAA Change a Concern to Parents," *Christianity Today Entertainment*, September 4, 2009. http://blog.christianitytoday.com.
Caroline Fredrickson	"Why Government Should Not Police TV Violence and Indecency," *Christian Science Monitor*, September 6, 2007. www .csmonitor.com.
John Hudston	"Regulating Violent Video Games: A Job for Parents or Government?," *AtlanticWire*, April 27, 2010. www .theatlanticwire.com.
PBS	"Federal Government Calls for Regulation of TV Violence," May 2, 2007. www.pbs.org.
Adam D. Thierer	"Should We Regulate Violent TV?," *City Journal*, vol. 21, no. 4, Autumn 2011. www.city-journal.org.
Shankar Vendantam	"It's a Duel; How Do Violent Video Games Affect Kids?," NPR, July 7, 2011. www.npr.org.
Wall Street Journal	"Should the FCC Curb TV Violence?," May 21, 2007. http:// online.wsj.com.

What Is the Effect of Violence in the News?

Chapter Preface

Local news in the United States is often filled with stories about crime; national news is often filled with stories about war. One form of violence that is not seen directly on the news, however, is executions. In 2010 the United States executed forty-six people, but those executions were not shown live to the public.

In a July 29, 2011, *New York Times* article, Zachary B. Shemtob and David Lat argue that executions should be televised. They reason that executions are a public act, and as such should be open to public viewing. "Our focus is on accountability and openness," they write. "A democracy demands a citizenry as informed as possible about the costs and benefits of society's ultimate punishment."

Some people maintain that broadcasting executions would be a step toward eliminating the death penalty. Sister Helen Prejean, an anti-death penalty advocate, argues in a May 1, 2001, article on *Good Morning America*'s website that the execution of Oklahoma City bomber Timothy McVeigh should have been televised. In the GMA article, she says, "If the public could see what it means . . . the consequences to take a human being who's alive and take him into a room, or her, and kill them—I think we'll end the death penalty sooner."

On the other side are those who assert that televising executions would negatively impact society. Some believe it would be barbaric, while others believe it would make the public desensitized to the death penalty. A recent controversy around this issue occurred in 2011, when the execution of Andrew DeYoung in Georgia was videotaped in order to gather evidence as to whether lethal injection was a cruel punishment. Prosecutors opposed the recording because they said it would threaten security. DeYoung's attorney believed that the tape should not have been made public, stating, "It's a horrible thing that Andrew DeYoung had to go through, and it's not for the public to see."

Authors in the following chapter offer differing viewpoints on the effect violence in the news has on society.

| "Round-the-clock coverage of child abductions, war, terrorism, and even hurricanes has made it difficult to shield young children from graphic news stories."

Violence in the News Increases Children's Fear and Anxiety

Barbara J. Wilson

Barbara J. Wilson is the head of the Department of Communication at the University of Illinois at Urbana-Champaign. In the following viewpoint, she says that there is evidence that high levels of media exposure among young children are linked to increased anxiety. In particular, she says, children who view news stories about violent events such as terrorism or kidnapping experience higher levels of anxiety. She adds that this anxiety is not just a temporary effect, but seems to last a long time and affects children's view of the world.

As you read, consider the following questions:

1. According to Wilson, a survey found what effects among children who watched television before bedtime?

Barbara J. Wilson, "Media and Children's Aggression, Fear, and Altruism," *The Future of Children*, Spring 2008, vol. 1, pp. 92–97. From *The Future of Children*, a collaboration of The Woodrow Wilson School of Public and International Affairs at Princeton University and the Brookings Institution. Reproduced by permission.

2. In general, under what circumstances are children's fear reactions to the news increased, according to Wilson?

3. How does Wilson say that the media sensationalize kidnapping?

Children can not only witness and share emotions experienced by media characters, but also respond directly to emotionally charged events depicted in the media. Much of the research on the media's capacity to evoke children's emotions has focused narrowly on its ability to arouse their fears and anxieties. Recent movies such as *Monster House, Corpse Bride*, and *Harry Potter and the Order of the Phoenix* are just a few examples of horror-filled content that is targeted to children. Classic Disney films such as *Bambi, Snow White*, and *The Lion King* can also be upsetting to very young children. Even programs not designed to be scary sometimes cause fear among younger age groups. *The Incredible Hulk*, for example, a television series featuring a large, green-skinned creature that helps people, was so frightening to preschoolers that *Mister Rogers' Neighborhood* screened a special segment to explain the Hulk's motives and make-up to young viewers.

Media, Fear, and Anxiety

Research shows that most preschoolers and elementary school children have experienced short-term fright reactions to the media. Furthermore, many of these children report that they regret having seen a particular scary program or movie. In one nationally representative survey, 62 percent of parents of two- to seventeen-year-olds agreed that their children had "sometimes become scared that something they saw in a movie or on TV might happen to them." The more pressing question concerns the long-term ramifications of such emotional reactions.

Evidence is growing that the fear induced in children by the media is sometimes severe and long-lasting. A survey of more than 2,000 elementary and middle school children revealed that heavy television viewing was associated with self-reported symptoms of anxiety, depression, and post-traumatic stress. Watching more than six hours of television a day put children at greater risk for scoring in the clinical range of these trauma symptoms. A survey of nearly 500 parents of elementary school children found that the children who watched television just before bedtime had greater difficulty falling asleep, were more anxious at bedtime, and had higher rates of nightmares. It is difficult to draw firm causal conclusions from these studies, which simply correlate television watching and anxiety, but it seems more likely that heavy watching would trigger fearfulness than that skittish children would seek out television before bedtime.

Using a different approach, Kristen Harrison and Joanne Cantor interviewed a sample of 150 college students at two universities about their memories of intense fears related to the media. A full 90 percent of the students were able to describe in detail a movie or television program that had frightened them in a lasting way. Although most had seen the show during childhood or adolescence, 26 percent reported still experiencing "residual anxiety" as an adult. When questioned about long-term effects, more than half of the sample (52 percent) reported disturbances in sleep or eating after seeing the TV show or movie. In addition, 36 percent said they avoided real-life situations similar to the events depicted in the media, 22 percent reported being mentally preoccupied or obsessed with the frightening content, and 17 percent said they avoided similar movies or television programs. The researchers also found that the younger the child was at the time of the exposure, the longer the fear lasted.

The media content that upsets children varies by age. Preschoolers and younger elementary school children (two to seven years of age) are most frightened by characters and events that look or sound scary. Creatures such as ghosts, witches, and monsters are likely to provoke fear in younger children; even

Violence and News About Children on the Internet

These data represent the results of a Google news search for the term "child." Media coverage of children mostly focuses on violence. Children who view news coverage may see disturbing accounts of violence against children.

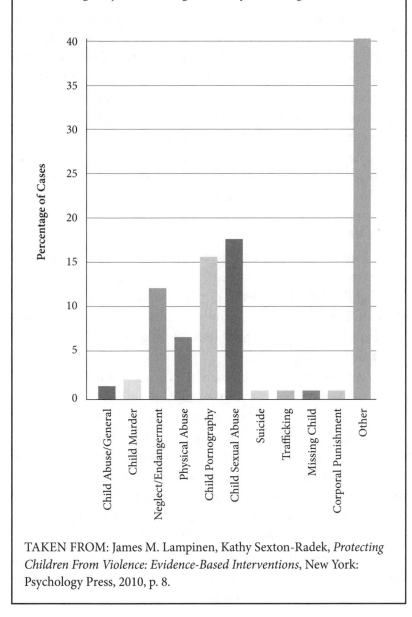

TAKEN FROM: James M. Lampinen, Kathy Sexton-Radek, *Protecting Children From Violence: Evidence-Based Interventions*, New York: Psychology Press, 2010, p. 8.

characters that are benign but visually grotesque, such as E.T., can be upsetting to a preschooler, much to the surprise of many parents. This pattern is consistent with younger children's perceptual dependence, their tendency to fixate on visual and auditory cues rather than more conceptual information such as the motives of a character. Older elementary school children (eight to twelve years of age) are frightened more by scenes involving injury, violence, and personal harm. Older children also are more responsive than younger children are to events in the media that seem realistic or could happen in real life. This heightened responsiveness is consistent with their more mature understanding of the distinction between fantasy and reality. Several studies have found, for example, that older children or tweens (age eight to twelve) are more frightened by television news than are younger children.

News and Anxiety

Catastrophic news events, in particular, have raised concerns among many parents in recent years. Round-the-clock coverage of child abductions, war, terrorism, and even hurricanes has made it difficult to shield young children from graphic news stories. Indeed, the content of television news has become more violent and graphic over time.

Several studies have found that exposure to news increases children's fear and anxiety. One study examined sixth graders suffering from post-traumatic stress disorder two years after the Oklahoma City bombing.[1] The disorder is characterized by intense fear, helplessness, horror, and disorganized or agitated behavior. The children in the study lived 100 miles away from the event, had no direct exposure to it, and knew no one affected by the bombing. Yet almost 20 percent reported that the event continued to cause them to have difficulty functioning at school or at home, or both, two years later. Moreover, children who had watched, listened to, or read more news about the bombing reported greater symptoms of post-traumatic stress.

Researchers have reported similar findings in the wake of the September 11 [2011] terrorist attacks [on the World Trade Center and the Pentagon]. One nationally representative survey of parents found that 35 percent of American children experienced one or more stress symptoms, such as difficulty falling asleep or trouble concentrating, after the attacks and that 47 percent were worried about their own safety or the safety of loved ones. Children who watched more TV coverage of the attacks had significantly greater stress symptoms.

In general, children's fear reactions to the news are intensified if they live in close geographic proximity to the tragedy. Fear is also greater among children who closely identify with the victims of tragic events. Finally, older elementary school children tend to be more frightened by these types of news stories than do younger children. Older children feel heightened fear partly because they watch more news than young children do. They are also more likely to be able to comprehend news stories, which often contain abstract terminology, such as terrorism and abduction, and fewer visuals than fictional, entertainment media content does. But as with fictional content, developmental differences help explain which types of news stories children find frightening. Although children under the age of eight are less likely to be scared of the news, when they are, it is most often in response to stories with graphic and intense visual images, such as natural disasters and accidents. Older children are more likely to be upset by stories involving crime and violence.

To summarize, a moderate amount of evidence links media exposure, both to fictional content and to the news, with children's fears and anxieties. Cross-sectional snapshot-in-time studies indicate that most children have experienced fright, sometimes intense and enduring, in response to media content. Experimental studies corroborate that the types of content that upset children vary as a function of age. Children under eight are most often frightened by fantasy portrayals that involve gruesome or ugly-looking characters. Children older than eight are more upset by realistic portrayals, including the news, involving personal injury and violence. Fear reactions differ by gender as well. Girls tend to experience more fear from media than boys do, especially as they get older. But gender differences are more pronounced for self-reported fear than for physical measures of fear, such as facial expressions. Thus, gender differences may reflect socialization differences among girls and boys.

Longitudinal evidence also links media and fear. Heavy exposure to major catastrophes in the news is associated with intense fear and even post-traumatic stress in children. But although most of the longitudinal [that is, from studies that follow people over a long period of time] evidence pertains to news events, one recent study suggests that television viewing in general may be linked to children's fear. Jeffrey Johnson and several colleagues followed the television viewing habits and sleep problems of a cohort of adolescents at age fourteen, sixteen, and twenty-two. Those who watched three or more hours of television daily at age fourteen were significantly more likely than lighter viewers to have trouble falling asleep and to wake frequently at night at ages sixteen and twenty-two. The link held true even after researchers controlled for previous sleep problems, psychiatric disorders, and parental education, income, and neglect. And the link ran only one way: sleep problems in the early years did not predict greater television viewing in later years. The study, however, did not assess *what* the teens were watching on television. Clearly, more longitudinal studies are needed on how exposure to different types of fictional and nonfictional media content affects children's fears and worries.

Cultivating a Fear of Victimization

Media can also contribute to long-term fear through cultivation —its influence on people's conceptions of social reality. According to cultivation theory, people who watch a great deal of television will come to perceive the real world as being consistent with what they see on the screen. Cultivation theory has been applied to many types of reality beliefs, but much of the focus has been on perceptions about violence.

Researchers' preoccupation with violence is partly owing to the prevalence of aggression in American media. Large-scale studies of television programming, for example, have documented that nearly two out of three programs contain some physical violence. Moreover, a typical hour of television features an average of six different violent exchanges between perpetrators and victims. The extent of violence in programs targeted to children is even higher; 70 percent of children's shows contain violence, with an average of fourteen violent interchanges an hour.

How does all this violence affect people's perceptions of reality? Studies have found that frequent viewers of television, no matter what their age, see the world as a more dangerous place and are more frightened of being a victim of violence than infrequent viewers are. Most of the evidence is correlational [that is, it shows a link, but not necessarily causation], but a few experiments using control groups show that repeated exposure to television violence increases people's fear of victimization. Combining all the evidence, Michael Morgan and James Shanahan conducted a meta-analysis of published studies on cultivation that combined all the individual studies to get an aggregate numerical effect size. . . . Morgan and Shanahan found that television had a small but statistically significant effect on people's perceptions of violence. The effect was slightly larger for adults than for children, but because fewer studies involved younger age groups, this finding may not be reliable.

Early cultivation research focused on the sheer number of hours that people watch television, based on the assumption that violent content is formulaic and pervasive regardless of what is viewed. More recently, scholars have begun looking at particular types of genres, especially the news. In one study, elementary school children who frequently watched the news believed there were more murders in a nearby city than did infrequent viewers, even when researchers controlled for grade level, gender, exposure to fictional media violence, and overall TV viewing. Another survey found that children and teens who were heavy viewers of the news were more frightened by high-profile child kidnapping stories such as the Elizabeth Smart case than were light viewers of the news.[2] Heavy viewers of the news were also personally more worried about being abducted than light viewers were, even after researchers controlled for the child's age and gender as well as for parental news viewing and parental fear of abduction. Children's fear of kidnapping was not related to overall television exposure, only to news viewing.

Kidnapping in the News

Kidnapping is one news topic that the media tend to sensationalize. Since the late 1990s, the number of stories about child kidnapping in the news has been on the rise. Yet kidnapping constitutes less than 2 percent of all violent crimes in the United States targeted at children under the age of eighteen. Moreover, children are far more likely to be abducted by someone they know than by a stranger. In 1997, for example, 40 percent of juvenile kidnappings were perpetrated by a family member, 27 percent by an acquaintance, and 24 percent by a stranger. A very small fraction of abductions are what the FBI calls "stereotypical" kidnapping cases involving a child taken overnight and transported over some distance to be kept or killed. Despite these statistics, there has been a rash of stories in the news about stranger kidnappings. Dramatic programs such as NBC's *Kidnapped* and USA's *America's Most Wanted* also focus on abduction. These fictional and nonfictional stories may attract viewers, but they can also fuel an exaggerated fear of violence in young children.

To summarize, researchers have found modest evidence that electronic media can influence children's perceptions of how dangerous the world is. This effect is particularly evident among children who watch a great deal of news programming. Most of the evidence, however, is correlational, not causal, and is a snapshot of its subjects at one time. To date, no longitudinal research has tracked children over time to determine the long-term effects of such exposure on children's perceptions of social reality.

Notes

1. In 1995 anti-federal-government terrorists Timothy McVeigh, Terry Nichols, and others bombed a federal building in Oklahoma City, killing 168 people.
2. Elizabeth Smart was fourteen years old when she was abducted from her home in Salt Lake City, Utah, in 2002. She was found nine months later, and her kidnappers were arrested.

"*More than 4,000 American troops have died to protect their country from Saddam Hussein's non-existent weapons of mass destruction, but you'd never know it from the nightly news.*"

The Horrors of War Must Not Be Censored

Dan Kennedy

In the following viewpoint, professor Dan Kennedy says the President George W. Bush administration prevented photographers from showing images of the Iraq War. He argues that the censorship was meant to aid the campaign of Republican presidential candidate John McCain, who supported the war. Kennedy says that if images of war were available, opposition to the war might have solidified and hurt McCain's presidential chances. Kennedy argues that it is important for Americans to see the result of US policy in Iraq. Kennedy is an assistant professor of journalism at Northeastern University in Boston.

As you read, consider the following questions:

1. Who is Zoriah Miller, and what is his plight, according to Kennedy?

2. What does Kennedy say has become an article of faith on the political right?

3. What effect did images of war have during World War II and why did they have that effect, according to Kennedy?

E ven by the squeamish standards of the American media, the photographic record of the war in Iraq is remarkably antiseptic. The paradigmatic images are not of combat or of bodies in the street but, rather, the digital snapshots taken by US soldiers of Iraqi prisoners being humiliated at Abu Ghraib [a prison in Iraq where US soldiers tortured prisoners]—that is, a consequence of war rather than the thing itself.

War Photos

To an extent not appreciated by the public, the shortage of photographs depicting the dead and dying is not an accident. This past Saturday [July 2008], the *New York Times* reported on the plight of Zoriah Miller, a freelance photographer who was banned from covering the Marines because he posted several photos of their dead bodies on his website. Miller, the *Times* added, is hardly alone in being pressured not to show the world anything too graphic.

Questions about war photos are as old as photography itself. More than a century ago, Mathew Brady and other photographers shocked a nation with their images of dead soldiers in the American Civil War.

More recently, it has become an article of faith on the political right that grisly images of the Vietnam War—including the famous pictures of a street-side execution and of a naked young girl running from a napalm attack—undermined public support and led to the American defeat. Subsequent administrations have made it increasingly difficult for journalists to cover war in all its horror.

That effort has reached its nadir during the presidency of George [W.] Bush. And though its roots lay in the White House's desperate attempts to maintain some level of support for its failed policies, its censorious campaign is now being waged on behalf of Bush's preferred successor, John McCain [the Republican presidential candidate in 2008]. Unpopular as the war is, it would be more unpopular still if the public could truly see it.

Think back to the early, triumphant days of the Iraq war, leading up to the "Mission Accomplished" fiasco [when President Bush declared the war over in 2003 despite ongoing violence]. War was reduced to a video game, with action figures racing through the desert and streaks of light aimed toward Baghdad [Iraq's capital]. Once the insurgency began, the war became so dangerous for journalists to cover that they became dependent on the American military units with which they were embedded [that is, journalists were attached to specific military units]—a very different scenario from Vietnam, where reporters and photographers were able to operate with little interference.

More than 4,000 American troops have died to protect their country from Saddam Hussein's non-existent weapons of mass destruction, but you'd never know it from the nightly news. In a break with longstanding tradition, the White House even banned the media from observing the flag-draped coffins of dead soldiers when they arrive at Dover Air Force Base, in Delaware.

Photographs and Public Support

Contrary to conventional wisdom, bloody images of war do not necessarily undermine public support. I recently had an opportunity to view newsreel footage from the second world war, and a silent clip from the first world war, that were astonishingly graphic in their depiction of violence suffered by both the good guys and the bad guys.

The difference is that the second world war, especially, enjoyed near-universal popular support. Terrible images of troops felled in a war for survival only toughened the national resolve. Images of dead American troops in Iraq, by contrast, would—

Embedded Reporting on War and Critical Distance

Both the immediacy of embedded reporting and the report-ers' identification with the soldiers protecting them make it difficult for viewers to get any critical distance on events. Em-bedded reporting thereby turns real events into media events and produces a confusing effect on the viewer who is pulled into the action as if watching a war movie. The new wireless technology that allows soldiers and reporters to broadcast live from the front lines makes the coverage seem more like a war movie than a news report of a real one. The combina-tion of proximity in space and the real-time reporting work to isolate a particular space and time, extract it from its con-text, and present it as immediate, part of the eternal present of television, thereby evacuating its historical meaning.

Kelly Oliver, Women as Weapons of War:
Iraq, Sex, and the Media. *New York: Columbia
University Press, 2007, pp. 82–83.*

---

like those pictures from Vietnam—only serve to deepen public anger.

Just before I wrote this, I paged through a book of Iraq war photos by Ashley Gilbertson called *Whiskey Tango Foxtrot.* Gilbertson, whose pictures have often appeared in the *New York Times,* is not one to indulge in violence for violence's sake. There is as much blood and death in the brief slide show of Zoriah Miller's work as there is in all 264 pages of Gilbertson's book.

Still Gilbertson's images are difficult to look at because they are so real. His is not the Iraq of General David Petraeus [head of coalition forces in Iraq], [Iraqi] Prime Minister Nouri al-Maliki and the surge-emboldened Sunni Awakening.[1] Rather, we see courageous American troops, terrified civilians and an oppressive, overwhelming sense that it's all going to end badly. Gilbertson closes with the 2005 Iraqi elections, itself a bitter-sweet victory. He, and we, know that some of the worst violence occurred later on.

As it occurs still. On Monday, at least 53 people were killed and another 240 wounded in separate suicide attacks in Baghdad and Kirkuk [another Iraqi city]. McCain can repeat "the surge is working" as much as he likes. Iraq remains an incredibly danger-ous and fragile country.

Interviewers frequently ask [Democratic presidential can-didate and later president] Barack Obama if he'll admit he was wrong about the surge, but they rarely ask McCain if he was wrong about the war. In large measure that is because the American public cannot see the full consequences of this tragic mistake—a mistake that McCain supported from the beginning.

Note

1. The surge was an increase in US troops in 2007. The Sunni Awakening was a move-ment by Iraqi groups to unite for security and against terrorism.

> *"The American people are tired of walking on eggshells to placate a violent ideology."*

Osama bin Laden's Death Photo Should Be Released

Jimmie L. Foster

In the following viewpoint, veteran Jimmie L. Foster argues that President Barack Obama should release photographs of Osama bin Laden, a terrorist leader who was killed by US forces. Foster argues that the American people have suffered greatly from the war on terror. He also says that the United States should not limit freedom of expression for fear of the reprisals of Islamic terrorists. Foster is the national commander of the American Legion, a wartime veterans organization.

As you read, consider the following questions:

1. What does Foster believe creates a national security risk?
2. If showing the photographs is not about gathering trophies, what does Foster say it is about?
3. What conspiracy theories does Foster believe the photographs will help debunk?

Osama bin Laden [leader of the terrorist group al Qaeda that was responsible for the 9/11 attacks] is dead. Of that, I have no doubt.

The American People Paid

To question this statement one would have to question the skill and bravery of the Navy SEALS and believe that the master terrorist who occasionally appears in propaganda videos and audio recordings is capable of perpetually eluding all human and technological intelligence.

The unparalleled success of Sunday's [May 2011] mission makes President [Barack] Obama's decision to not release the bin Laden "death photographs" especially confounding. When an event organizer cut off the sound to candidate Ronald Reagan during a debate with George H.W. Bush, Reagan famously said, "I paid for this microphone!"

Well, Mr. President, the American people paid for those photographs. More than a trillion dollars, in fact, if you factor in the cost of the Department of Homeland Security, two wars, and the care for more than 40,000 veterans who have been wounded in Afghanistan and Iraq [both of which were invaded in response to the 9/11 attacks].

President Obama said that "given the graphic nature of these photos it would create a national security risk." I respectfully disagree.

Radical Islam creates the national security risk. There were no photographs that prompted the attacks on 9/11, the missile strike on the USS Cole or the bombing of the U.S. Marine barracks in Lebanon.[1] Does anyone seriously believe that the terrorists will hate us less if the photos are not released than they already do now?

Will the "death to America" chants that have existed since the Iranian hostage crisis [when Iranian militants held fifty-two Americans hostage from 1979 to 1981] suddenly morph into love sonnets?

The American people are tired of walking on eggshells to placate a violent ideology that respects neither innocent civilians nor the amazing humanitarian work performed by our soldiers every day. The problem is not blasphemous cartoons or even misguided pastors burning Korans.[2]

No Exceptions to Freedom of Speech

Where does the First Amendment include exception clauses for cases that might incite radical Islamists?

My organization, The American Legion, does not rejoice at any death. But let us remember what bin Laden has wrought. He is the reason more than 6,000 U.S. military families have buried loved ones lost in combat since 9/11. He is the reason our children are now groped in airports by security officials. He is the reason that the level of mistrust between the overwhelming majority of peaceful Muslims and those of other faiths exists.

It is not about gathering trophies or "spiking the football," as the president mischaracterized it. It's about showing a replay to season ticket holders who were barred from entering the stadium.

The photos are no doubt bloody and graphic. But do you know what else is painful to see? The burns on the faces of patients at Walter Reed Army Medical Center. Or the eyes of Michael Nordmeyer, the father of 21-year-old Zach Nordmeyer, a soldier and member of The American Legion who was killed in Iraq two years ago. It still pains most of us to look at images of firefighters running into the World Trade Center for the very last time.

There will be some who doubt the official version of bin Laden's death whether the photographs are released or not. But not releasing this evidence would surely be adding steroids to these nonsensical conspiracy theories.

Some say the photographs will bring closure. Others see it as a need to satisfy a thirst for vengeance. I prefer to think of them as symbols of justice. The raid on bin Laden's hide-out is a truly great moment in American history.

Mr. President, release the photographs. We paid an enormous price for them.

Notes

1. Al Qaeda attacked the World Trade Center and other US targets on September 11, 2001. It attacked the USS Cole in October 2000. Another terrorist organization bombed the Lebanon US Marine barracks in 1983.
2. Anti-Islamic cartoons published by a Danish newspaper sparked worldwide Muslim protests and violence in 2005. In 2010 a Florida pastor sparked international outrage when he threatened to burn 200 copies of the Koran.

> "Releasing the pictures of a dead bin
> Laden would have simply played to
> and reinforced the spirit of vengeance
> and prurient bloodlust."

Osama bin Laden's Death Photo Should Not Be Released

Earl Ofari Hutchinson

In the following viewpoint, columnist Earl Ofari Hutchinson contends there was no need to release pictures of the dead terrorist leader Osama bin Laden, because there was conclusive proof of his death. Hutchinson says releasing photos might have caused a Muslim backlash against US troops. Most importantly, Hutchinson argues releasing the photos would encourage a public expression of bloodlust, and this would be undignified and unworthy of the United States. Hutchinson is an author, syndicated columnist, and political commentator.

As you read, consider the following questions:

1. According to Hutchinson, what values does true patriotism extol?
2. What did President Obama say the killing of Osama bin Laden was *not*, according to Hutchinson?

Earl Ofari Hutchinson, "Releasing the Bin Laden Photos Would Have Turned the Killing Into a Voyeuristic Sideshow," *American Chronicle*, May 4, 2011. Copyright © 2011 by Earl Ofari Hutchinson. All rights reserved. Reproduced by permission.

3. What does Hutchinson believe critics will say they have been cheated out of by Obama's refusal to release the bin Laden pictures?

President [Barack] Obama made the only decision that makes any sense in deciding not to release the photos of the body of [leader of the terrorist group al Qaeda, Osama] bin Laden. That decision though based on pragmatism, namely that the DNA and other evidence was conclusive that it was bin Laden, and that if they released the photos it wouldn't satisfy the professional Obama bashers who would just claim that the photos were doctored anyway, and that release could inflame some Muslim hardliners who might take retaliatory action against US personnel. These are pragmatic and compelling reasons for not showing the gruesome kill.

Justice, Not Vengeance

But there is another reason that Obama did not state. The wild, and frankly, repelling scenes of some Americans shouting, dancing in the streets and high fiving the death of Osama was not a celebration of patriotism or emotional catharsis that Osama was dead. True patriotism celebrates and extols the values of tolerance, diversity, freedom of expression, and a denunciation of bigotry. The avalanche of racist tweets, and racial epithets from some bloggers, and the gloats from some rightwing talk show hosts, mocked true American patriotism. The supposed joy and relief that countless Americans said they felt and that the polls reflected at bin Laden's take down, had little to do with their emotional connection or even interest in bin Laden. He had been on the lam for a decade, and his name had long ceased to be an object of daily mention, or seeming concern by the [George W.] Bush administration and much of the media. Apart from the families, friends and associates of the thousands killed in the 9/11 terror attacks, and the trauma and emotional scars they carried from the deaths of their loved ones, bin Laden was little

Public Opinion on the Release of the Osama bin Laden Death Photos

Opinion	Percentage Agree
Believe the photos should have been released	5%
Strongly believe the photos should have been released	24%
Believe the photos should *not* have been released	12%
Strongly believed the photos should *not* have been released	52%

TAKEN FROM: Mark Murray, "NBC Poll: Nearly Two-Thirds Back Decision Not to Release bin Laden Photos," First Read—MSNBC.com, May 8, 2011. http://firstread.msnbc.msn.com.

more than a name from the past to most Americans. And that was particularly true of college students who seemed to use the news of bin Laden's death as more of a campus cheer session, pep rally and party, than an expression of any serious concern, let alone understanding, of what bin Laden and 9/11 really meant.

President Obama understood that and was careful to place the Osama killing as a national security priority, in the overall framework of the war on terrorism. He took great pains to add that the killing was not a war on Muslims, and that this should not be used as an excuse to finger point Muslims. Releasing the pictures of a dead bin Laden would have simply played to and reinforced the spirit of vengeance and prurient bloodlust that unfortunately is still much a part of the thinking of far too many Americans.

Avoid a Degrading Spectacle

It would have reduced the killing to that of a gladiator joust in which kills are measured by the amount of bodily mayhem the combatants can wreak on each other. This would make the bin Laden killing simply a freak, sideshow spectacle, and totally negate the point of why the US went after him in the first place. True, part of it was to see that justice was done. But part of it was also pure vengeance for the 9/11 attacks. But Obama smartly was careful not to publicly feed into that in his announcement that bin Laden was dead.

In the days to come, Obama will hear the loud chorus from many quarters that Americans deserved to have a parade of the bloody pictures of bin Laden splattered in front of them as their trophy for the kill. And there will be endless criticism that by not releasing the pictures this in some way deprives the country of having final satisfaction in seeing the corpse of their number one terror nemesis to gawk at, and this cheats the country of real closure.

It does no such thing. The killing of bin Laden brought a close to one sad, tragic, and painful episode in American history. That should be satisfaction enough. The photos of his corpse would turn the satisfaction many feel at the removal of bin Laden into a cheap, voyeuristic and degrading spectacle.

Periodical and Internet Sources Bibliography

The following articles have been selected to supplement the diverse views presented in this chapter.

Tom Fitton
"Obama Refuses to Release bin Laden Death Photos," *Big Government*, May 10, 2011. http://biggovernment.com.

Philip Gourevitch
"Don't Release the Photos," *New Yorker*, May 3, 2011. www.newyorker.com.

Kidshealth.org
"How to Talk to Your Child About the News," n.d. http://kidshealth.org.

Bryan Koenig
"'Most Wanted' Reporter Savors Catching Criminals," *The Eagle*, March 25, 2007. www.theeagleonline.com.

Media Awareness Network
"Media Crime Facts," n.d. www.media-awareness.ca.

Brian Montopli
"Obama: I Won't Release bin Laden Death Photos," CBS News, May 4, 2011. www.cbsnews.com.

Mark Pasetsky
"Osama Bin Laden Death Photo: Why It Must Be Released," *Forbes*, May 2, 2011. www.forbes.com.

Photography.com
"War Photography and Combat Photography," n.d. www.photography.com.

Steve Proffitt
"Photos of War: Censorship or Sensibility?," *KCET*, April 8, 2010. www.kcet.org.

JH van der Molen and BJ Bushman
"Children's Direct Fright and Worry Reactions to Violence in Fiction and News Television Programs," *Journal of Pediatrics*, vol. 153, no. 3, September 2008, pp. 420–424.

What Is the Relationship Between Violence and Sex in the Media?

Chapter Preface

Young adult (YA) novels aimed at teens and tweens often contain themes of sex and violence. In some cases, these themes provoke criticism. Megan Cox Gurdon, in a June 4, 2011, editorial in the *Wall Street Journal*, argues that "kidnapping and pederasty and incest and brutal beatings are now just part of the run of things in novels directed, broadly speaking, at children from the ages of 12 to 18." Gurdon worries these books might "normalize" such pathologies, and she argues that parents should hold the book industry accountable for its dangerous content.

Others have defended the violence and sexual content in YA books. In a June 5, 2011, essay on the site *Booking Through 365*, a teen blogger named Emma insists that YA fiction accurately represents the darker parts of teen lives, such as parental alcoholism, rape, and bullying. She maintains that "Good literature rips open all the private parts of us—the parts people like you have deemed too dark, inappropriate, grotesque or abnormal for teens to be feeling—and then they stitch it all back together again before we even realize they're not talking about us. They're talking about their characters."

Similarly, Andrea Cremer, a YA novelist, writes in an October 28, 2010, *Wall Street Journal* article that teens do not need to be shielded from real life in YA fiction. Instead, she says, the acknowledgement of the problems of violence and sexuality "can provide comfort, healing, or simply the realization that one isn't alone."

Cremer also notes that parents are often more comfortable with violence in YA books than they are with sex. Cremer argues that while the United States may have a long tradition of discomfort with sexuality, both sex and violence are valid themes in YA books. However, Larissa Ione, another YA author, expresses sympathy for parents who are more comfortable with violence than sex. She points out that most kids have little attraction to committing violence, but it is normal for boys and girls to eventually become interested in sex. Ione concludes that parents who are okay with violence but not sex may think, "'I know my kid isn't going to go on a killing rampage, but sex is normal and fun . . . and it's not time for him/her to deal with that yet.'"

The authors in the following chapter offer various opinions on the relationship between sex and violence in the media.

> *"If the claimed harmful effects of minors' exposure to violence, gore and racism do not warrant a governmental limitation on free speech, why isn't sexually prurient material . . . deserving of equal First Amendment protection?"*

Yes to Violence, No to Sex

Robert Scheer

Robert Scheer is the editor in chief of Truthdig. *In the following viewpoint, he discusses the Supreme Court's decision to prevent California from regulating violent video games on First Amendment grounds. Scheer applauds the Court's defense of free speech, but argues that if violent material is not regulated, sexual material should not be regulated either. Scheer concludes that Americans are more comfortable with violence than sex, which he suggests is illogical and unhealthy.*

As you read, consider the following questions:

1. What specifically did the California law prohibit, according to Scheer?

2. Why, in Scheer's opinion, is Justice Scalia's view a vast improvement over that of Justice Clarence Thomas?
3. According to Scheer, on what grounds did Justice Scalia dismiss Justice Alito's concerns about violent video games?

This American life of ours has long been pro-violence and anti-sex, unless the two can be merged so that violence is the dominant theme. The U.S. Supreme Court reaffirmed that historical record on Monday in declaring California's ban on the sale of violent video games to minors unconstitutional while continuing to deny constitutional protection to purely prurient sexual material for either minors or adults.

The California law that the court struck down prohibited the sale or rental of violent games to minors "in which the range of options available to a player includes killing, maiming, dismembering, or sexually assaulting an image of a human being," unless the work, taken as a whole, possessed redeeming literary, artistic or social value—qualities that limit censorship of sexually "obscene" material.

The Supreme Court, in essence, said no—"sexually assaulting an image of a human being" is protected speech, but depicting graphic sexual activity that is nonviolent and consensual is not.

"California has tried to make violent-speech regulation look like obscenity regulation by appending a saving clause required for the latter," Justice Antonin Scalia wrote in the majority opinion. "That does not suffice. Our cases have been clear that the obscenity exception to the First Amendment does not cover whatever a legislature finds shocking, but only depictions of 'sexual conduct.'"

As Scalia put the prevailing argument that says yes to violence and no to sex, it is only violence that possesses deep cultural roots going back to our favorite fairy tales. Arguing that "violence is not part of the obscenity that the Constitution permits to be

regulated," Scalia made clear that the problem is with the sex and not the violent or misogynist behavior that some critics argue will result from material the court defines as obscene: "Because speech about violence is not obscene, it is of no consequence that California's statute mimics the New York statute regulating obscenity-for-minors that we upheld in *Ginsberg v. New York*. That case approved a prohibition on the sale to minors of *sexual* material that would be obscene from the perspective of a child."

Scalia's opinion is actually quite thrilling in enunciating an extremely broad definition of the free speech rights of minors. But it is simply bizarre in dismissing the claimed harmful effects of violent depictions while still insisting on the strictest puritanical view of the dangers of sexual imagery. "No doubt a State possesses legitimate power to protect children from harm, but that does not include a free-floating power to restrict the ideas to which children may be exposed," he said. Unless sex is involved, in which case, as Scalia quotes an earlier court decision: "Speech that is neither obscene as to youths nor subject to some other legitimate proscription cannot be suppressed solely to protect the young from ideas or images that a legislative body thinks unsuitable for them."

In that regard, Scalia's view is a vast improvement over that of Clarence Thomas, who held in his dissent that minors have no First Amendment rights at all. But Scalia is unnerving in his dismissal of the concurring opinion of Justice Samuel Alito Jr., in which Chief Justice John Roberts joined. Alito argued that the California statute addressed "a potentially serious social problem" but that "its terms are not framed with the precision that the Constitution demands. . . ."

Scalia's withering dismissal of Alito's concerns is revealing of his tolerance for violent imagery as opposed to that which is merely sexual:

> Justice Alito has done considerable independent research to identify video games in which "the violence is astounding. . . . Victims are dismembered, decapitated, disemboweled, set on fire, and chopped into little pieces. . . . Blood gushes, splatters, and pools." Justice Alito recounts all these disgusting video games in order to disgust us—but disgust is not a valid basis for restricting expression. . . . Thus, ironically, Justice Alito's argument highlights the precise danger posed by the California Act: that the *ideas* expressed by speech—whether it be violence, or gore, or racism—and not its objective effects, may be the real reason for governmental proscription.

Hear, hear to such a bold defense of the right of minors to consider a full range of controversial thought, but if the claimed harmful effects of minors' exposure to violence, gore and racism do not warrant a governmental limitation on free speech, why isn't sexually prurient material—for adults if not minors—

deserving of equal First Amendment protection? The unspoken answer that runs through Scalia's opinion, and that of the court down through the ages, is that violence is normal while sex is obscene.

> *"Representations of women and men
> indeed have become more sexualized
> over time, and women continue to be
> more frequently sexualized than men."*

Americans Are Right to Worry More About Media Sex than Media Violence

USA Today (Magazine)

USA Today (Magazine) is a monthly periodical published by the Society for the Advancement of Education. The article argues that the sexualization of women in media has grown over the years. The authors state that media is not just depicting women as sexy musicians or actors, but rather as readily available for sex. This oversexualization of women has been found to legitimize violence against women and girls, according to the article.

As you read, consider the following questions:
1. What magazine did the researchers cited in this article use to measure the sexualization of women?
2. In the 2000s, what percentage of images of women were sexualized?
3. As stated in the article, does the sexualization of women in the media increase eating disorders?

The portrayal of women in the popular media over the last several decades has become increasingly sexualized, even "pornified," a study by University at Buffalo (N.Y.) sociologists contends. The same is not true of men. These findings may be cause for concern since previous research has found sexualized images of women to have far-reaching negative consequences for both sexes.

The researchers examined the covers of *Rolling Stone* magazine from 1967–2009 to measure changes in the sexualization of men and women in popular media over time. "We chose *Rolling Stone* because it is a well-established, pop-culture media outlet. It is not explicitly about sex or relationships; foremost it is about music—but it also covers politics, film, television, and current events, and so offers a useful window into how women and men are portrayed generally in popular culture," explains Erin Hatton, assistant professor in the department of sociology.

More Sexualized Representations of Men and Women in the Media

The authors concluded that representations of women and men indeed have become more sexualized over time, and women continue to be more frequently sexualized than men. In the 1960s, they found that 11% of men and 44% of women were sexualized. In the 2000s, 17% of men and 83% of women were sexualized. Among those images, two percent of men and 61% of women were hypersexualized.

"What we conclude from this is that popular media outlets such as *Rolling Stone* are not depicting women as sexy musicians or actors; they are depicting women musicians and actors as ready and available for sex. This is problematic because it indicates a decisive narrowing of media representations of women," Hatton stresses.

"We don't necessarily think it's problematic for women to be portrayed as 'sexy,' but we do think it is problematic when nearly all images of women depict them not simply as 'sexy women' but as passive objects for someone else's sexual pleasure.

History Provides the Basis to Regulate Media Sex But Not Media Violence

Images of violence are a fundamental part of our history, culture, and politics. Can we imagine censors reviewing films like *Saving Private Ryan* [a 1998 film about WWII] and *Schindler's List* [a 1993 film about the Holocaust] to determine whether their depictions of violence are of low First Amendment value? Can we imagine censors making it a crime for *Time* magazine or CNN to show images of terrorist beheadings or of Mai Lai [a 1968 massacre of Vietnamese by US troops] because such depictions are thought to offend contemporary community standards?

Of course, we allow just that in the realm of sex. But that is precisely why history is relevant. At least with obscenity, we have managed over many years to develop reasonably workable standards. To start from scratch in the realm of violence, after eschewing that approach for more than two centuries, would open a Pandora's box that is both unnecessary and unwise.

Geoffrey R. Stone, "Sex, Violence, and the First Amendment," University of Chicago Law Review, *vol. 74, 2007, pp. 1866–1867.*

"Sexualized portrayals of women have been found to legitimize or exacerbate violence against women and girls, as well as sexual harassment and anti-women attitudes among men and boys. Such images also have been shown to increase rates of body dissatisfaction and/or eating disorders among men, women, and girls, as well as decrease sexual satisfaction among both men and women."

| "Our kids are surrounded by these brutal representations of girls and women, and it is no wonder that women and young girls are the victims of male violence."

Sexualized Violence in the Media Contributes to Violence Against Women

Marina DelVecchio

In the following viewpoint, teacher Marina DelVecchio argues that sexualized images of beaten or dead women encourage real violence against women. She points to music videos, television, fashion, and comic books to show evidence of the pervasiveness of images of sexualized violence. DelVecchio is a teacher and a contributing writer to the New Agenda.

As you read, consider the following questions:
1. What does DelVecchio say that the Greek word *miso* means, and how does she apply this to the meaning of *misogyny*?
2. What images of violence against women does Anita

Marina DelVecchio, "The Media's Contribution to Violence Against Women," TheNew Agenda.net, April 10, 2011. Copyright © 2011 by Marina DelVecchio. All rights reserved. Reproduced by permission.

Sarkeesian say are used in Kanye West's music video for "Monster" on the *My Beautiful Dark Twisted Fantasy* album?

3. According to DelVecchio, what is the focus of Gail Simone's blog *Women in Refrigerators*?

Misogyny is defined as "hatred of women." Interestingly, *miso* in Greek not only means "hatred", it also means "half." If we apply this definition to the way women are presently being depicted in the media—in movies, television shows, cartoons, music videos, and even comic books—it is clear that women are presented as half-human and objectified. If a woman is looked upon as an object, without feelings, life, soul, or thoughts, then it is easy to ingest images of her that defy her humanity. She is not a woman—a living creature with human attributes. She is merely a body, a vacant, empty, vessel intended to contain the needs of others—preferably men—and her body, which is the most desired aspect of her existence, perfect, lithe, smooth and hair-free, is open for interpretation and domination.

Objectification Justifies Violence

Because she is half a woman, the acceptable and sexy parts of her—her eyes, her mouth, her breasts, her long legs, and her thighs and genitals—are coveted, defined, exploited, manipulated, and used to satiate men's needs, while the rest of her—her mind, intelligence, thoughts, and voice are avoided, silenced, and virtually non-existent. This type of misogyny exists in our culture—our refined, free, and progressive American culture. It is a prevailing theme perpetuated by corporations that dabble in pop culture's music, movies, reality television shows, and commercials, using female sex to make tons of cash. And while their pockets are filling with dough, women suffer the consequences of being dehumanized and objectified.

In [the article] "Two Ways a Woman Can Get Hurt," Jean Kilbourne claims that by "turning a human being into a thing, an object, is almost always the first step toward justifying violence against that person." She contends that by using female sex to sell their products, advertising companies send the message that "all women, regardless of age, are really temptresses in disguise, nymphets, sexually instable and seductive."

Advertising isn't the only culprit, however, which inarguably demonstrates that this attitude towards women and their dislocated, dislodged, dismembered bodies is a rampant theme.

It is in reality television shows. In an article published at *Women in Media and News*, Jennifer L. Pozner criticizes misogynist representations in popular reality TV shows such as *America's Next Top Model*, which just aired a challenge for their models to pretend they were dead and sexily clad: This misogyny has been manifesting itself in print for years as advertising's fetishization of images of beautifully beaten, raped, drugged, tortured and murdered girls . . . today, advertisers are advancing these same backwards notions in 3-D, in the name of "reality," their product placement bucks allowing them to influence and sometimes even control the dialog, sets, themes and plotlines of primetime's most popular "unscripted" programs.

Images of scantily clad and sexy women who are dead has become an artistic motif in music videos. Recently, Kanye West released a music video for [the song "Monster" on] his new album titled *My Beautiful Dark Twisted Fantasy* [2011], wherein images of beautiful but dead women are presented. Anita Sarkeesian, a pop culture media critic who creates video blogs for Feminist Frequency describes it quite well:

> Throughout the video we are presented with a series of lifeless, nearly naked, mutilated women's bodies. We see women, or parts of women, all white, draped across sofas, propped up in beds, hanging from nooses, and all with perfectly applied make up and high heels. In addition to the sexualized,

dismembered body parts, we're also treated to Kanye holding up a freshly severed head.

And as the title of Kanye's album points out, this is his "fantasy"—to be surrounded by the vacant bodies of sexy, fragmented women who look good, but have nothing to say—their bodies/corpses to be used in any way the man deems necessary in having his pleasures and fantasies satiated. Her body exists for him—without her actually being present. Very disturbing.

Not Creative Expression

This image of sexy corpses saturates also the artistic realms of fashion photography. *The Society Pages* posted an article by Gwen Sharp titled "More Sexualized Violence in Fashion," which shows very graphic and violent photos of models portrayed as dead, a few of them depicting the images of [actress] Lindsay Lohan holding a gun, having a gun aimed at her face, and lying on the floor, wearing barely anything, and surrounded by blood. . . .

Lohan and the photographer argue that this is creative expression, but it surely isn't. And if it is, then what are they creatively expressing—that violence and brutality become women? That it is OK and commonplace to fantasize over dead or brutalized women? That they're sexier and more erotic when they're dead, lying in a pool of their own blood?

And who sees these images? If you think your kids aren't, you are sadly mistaken. These images are everywhere. They're in places parents don't think to check, like on their cell phones, ipods, mp3s, and the computers they do their homework on. They're in the songs they listen to, the movies they see with their friends, the news that report gang rapes, rapes, murders of little girls, and pregnant women; they're even in comic books, as illustrated by Gail Simone's *Women In Refrigerators*, a blog that she created, which provides a lengthy list of female characters brutalized, raped, and/or murdered in order to drive the main male character in comic books to seek revenge for his beloved's death.

Our kids are surrounded by these brutal representations of girls and women, and it is no wonder that women and young girls are the victims of male violence. No wonder that 20% of college girls will be sexually assaulted by guys they know in school. And it is no wonder that boys as young as 14 are capable of raping little girls as young as 11. How else are they to perceive girls if they are inundated daily with images of half-humans, half-living women, looking "sick and sexified," as Kesha's new song ["We R Who We R," 2010] goes.

| "As raunch has waxed, rape has
| waned."

Pornography Does Not
Cause Rape

Steve Chapman

In the following viewpoint, columnist Steve Chapman contends that there is no evidence that pornography encourages rape. Instead, he argues, as the Internet has made it easier to access porn, rape and sexual violence have dropped significantly. Chapman says that Internet porn may be causing the drop by giving sexual predators a different outlet. Alternately, better education or anti-violence efforts may have caused the decrease. Either way, Chapman says, it is clear that more pornography has not caused more sexual violence. Chapman is an editorial writer for the Chicago Tribune.

As you read, consider the following questions:

1. Why does Chapman say that the campaign against pornography fizzled?
2. What statistics does Chapman provide to demonstrate that rape and sexual assault have decreased?
3. What technological advance does Chapman believe may be responsible for the decrease in sexual assaults?

In the 1980s, conservatives and feminists joined to fight a common nemesis: the spread of pornography. Unlike past campaigns to stamp out smut, this one was based not only on morality but also public safety. They argued that hard-core erotica was intolerable because it promoted sexual violence against women.

Anti-Pornography Activists Were Wrong

"Pornography is the theory; rape is the practice," wrote feminist author Robin Morgan. In 1986, a federal commission concurred. Some kinds of pornography, it concluded, are bound to lead to "increased sexual violence." Indianapolis passed a law allowing women to sue producers for sexual assaults caused by material depicting women in "positions of servility or submission or display."

The campaign fizzled when the courts said the ordinance was an unconstitutional form of "thought control." Though the [President George W.] Bush administration has put new emphasis on prosecuting obscenity, on the grounds that it fosters violence against women, pornography is more available now than ever.

That's due in substantial part to the rise of the Internet, where the United States alone has a staggering 244 million Web pages featuring erotic fare. One Nielsen survey found that one out of every four users say they visited adult sites in the last month.

So in the last two decades [starting in the late 1980s], we have conducted a vast experiment on the social consequences of such material. If the supporters of censorship were right, we should be seeing an unparalleled epidemic of sexual assault. But all the evidence indicates they were wrong. As raunch has waxed, rape has waned.

This is part of a broad decrease in criminal mayhem. Since 1993, violent crime in America has dropped by 58 percent. But the progress in this one realm has been especially dramatic. Rape is down 72 percent and other sexual assaults have fallen by 68 percent. Even in the last two years [2005–2007], when the

The Relationship Between Pornography and Sexual Assault

The effects of pornography, whether violent or non-violent, on sexual aggression have been debated for decades. The current review examines evidence about the influence of pornography on sexual aggression. . . . Evidence for a causal relationship between exposure to pornography and sexual aggression is slim and may, at certain times, have been exaggerated by politicians, pressure groups and some social scientists. Some of the debate has focused on violent pornography, but evidence of any negative effects is inconsistent, and violent pornography is comparatively rare in the real world. Victimization rates for rape in the United States demonstrate an inverse relationship between pornography consumption and rape rates [that is, as pornography consumption rises, rape rates fall]. Data from other nations have suggested similar relationships. Although these data cannot be used to determine that pornography has a cathartic effect on rape behavior, combined with the weak evidence in support of negative causal hypotheses from the scientific literature, it is concluded that it is time to discard the hypothesis that pornography contributes to increased sexual assault behavior.

> *Christopher J. Ferguson and Richard*
> *D. Hartley, "The Pleasure Is Momentary . . .*
> *The Expense Damnable?: The Influence of*
> *Pornography on Rape and Sexual Assault,"*
> Aggression and Violent Behavior, *vol. 14,*
> *no. 5, September–October 2009, p. 323.*

FBI reported upticks in violent crime, the number of rapes continued to fall.

Nor can the decline be dismissed as the result of underreporting. Many sexual assaults do go unreported, but there is no reason to think there is less reporting today than in the past. In fact, given everything that has been done to educate people about the problem and to prosecute offenders, victims are probably more willing to come forward than they used to be.

No one would say the current level of violence against women is acceptable. But the enormous progress in recent years is one of the most gratifying successes imaginable.

The Internet Reduces Rape

How can it be explained? Perhaps the most surprising and controversial account comes from Clemson University economist Todd Kendall, who suggests that adult fare on the Internet may essentially inoculate against sexual assaults.

In a paper presented at Stanford Law School last year [2006], he reported that, after adjusting for other differences, states where Internet access expanded the fastest saw rape decline the most. A 10 percent increase in Internet access, Kendall found, typically meant a 7.3 percent reduction in the number of reported rapes. For other types of crime, he found no correlation with Web use. What this research suggests is that sexual urges play a big role in the incidence of rape—and that pornographic Web sites provide a harmless way for potential predators to satisfy those desires.

That, of course, is only a theory, and the evidence he cites is not conclusive. States that were quicker to adopt the Internet may be different in ways that also serve to prevent rape. It's not hard to think of other explanations why sexual assaults have diminished so rapidly—such as DNA analysis, which has been an invaluable tool in catching and convicting offenders.

Changing social attitudes doubtless have also played a role. Both young men and young women are more aware today of the boundaries between consensual and coercive sex. Kim Gandy, president of the National Organization for Women, thinks the credit for progress against rape should go to federal funding under the Violence Against Women Act and to education efforts stressing that "no means no."

But if expanding the availability of hard-core fare doesn't prevent rapes, we can be confident from the experience of recent years that it certainly doesn't cause such crimes. Whether you think porn is a constitutionally protected form of expression or a vile blight that should be eradicated, this discovery should come as very good news.

> *"My views on the dangers of hip-hop
> began to change in 1997 when the great
> rapper Notorious BIG . . . was shot
> dead in California."*

Hip Hop and Hip-Hop Journalism Promote Violence

Sonia Poulton

In the following viewpoint, music journalist Sonia Poulton says that she used to defend hip hop from the charge that it incited violence. She was excited by hip hop's danger and she felt that criticism of it was racially motivated. After the violent deaths of several major hip-hop artists, however, she decided she had been guilty of romanticizing and promoting violence. She argues that journalists and rappers need to stop glorifying the gangsta lifestyle. Poulton is a reporter whose work has appeared in Q Magazine, The Independent, The Times, *and numerous other publications.*

As you read, consider the following questions:

1. Where did gangsta rap start, according to Poulton?
2. What songs does Poulton cite as examples of white rock artists glorifying violence?

3. What event does Poulton say prompted David Cameron's comments about the dangers of violent rap music?

D avid Cameron [then leader of the Tory Party in Britain] caused a stir when he told Radio 1 [the British public broadcasting station] recently: "Do you realise some of the stuff you play on Saturday nights encourages people to carry guns and knives?"

Guilt and Gangsta Rap

The Tory leader's attack on gangsta rap was directed at the BBC [the British Broadcasting Corporation, a public service broadcaster] but, as this debate has grown, I wonder if there were other journalists, PRs [public relations], television producers and radio executives out there who—like me—are feeling a little guilty about their own roles in promoting this music?

Gangsta rap emerged in the Eighties from the West Coast of America. It was rap's seamy underbelly and very different from the conscious polemics of the likes of Public Enemy over on the East Coast. It was my job, as a music journalist until the late-Nineties, to report on it for music and style magazines and newspapers. I also relayed tales of my adventures in rap-land for Kiss FM radio listeners every week. I was rewarded with unrivalled access to the biggest artists and the scoops that came with it.

I have discussed [rapper] Tupac Shakur's murder [in 1996] around [rapper and producer] P Diddy's dining table (he knew the rumours and denied involvement) and listened to a fearful [rapper] Snoop Doggy Dogg prior to his [1995–96] murder trial (he also claimed innocence and was acquitted).

My commitment to the hip-hop cause frequently found me caught up in the artist's personal skirmishes. I have wiped mace from the eyes of the Wu-Tang Clan's Raekwon and Ice Cube (real name O'Shea Jackson) has shown me bullet holes in his living room. His mother Hosea, meanwhile, has shown me his nice college photos and questioned why her son has made millions from rapping about "F--- Tha' Police." "I don't see my O'Shea saying those curse words. I see him like an actor," she told me. And an actor is what he later became.

As a white female from the Cotswolds [in West-Central England], hip-hop, and the promotion of it, may not have seemed like a natural vocation—but it suited me. Rap music and its inherent edginess spoke to my desire to live dangerously.

Race and Censorship

Racial inequality also motivated me. It seemed hip-hop—and by extension black people—was under attack. In America, the music-censorship lobby the Parent Music Resource Centre raged against rap and rock music and eventually triumphed with the emergence of the Parental Advisory stickers.

NWA (Niggaz with Attitude), arguably the first mainstream gangsta rappers, were investigated by the FBI for incitement to violence. And the subsequent furore over Ice-T's "Cop Killer"— in response to the brutal beating of Rodney King in 1991 by the LAPD [Los Angeles Police Department]—resulted in his release from Warner Brothers Records.

It seemed an uneven playing field. Eric Clapton's "I Shot the Sheriff" cover didn't outrage the public. And John Lennon's "Happiness is a Warm Gun" could be construed as glorifying guns. Apparently it was OK for white boys.

Today satellite and cable channels show rap videos of young, primarily black men swaggering, pack-like, through grimy estates, pulling imaginary triggers with their fingers. Young men who perceive violence as cool. Marketing executives, who grow rich from the sales of the brand-name hoodies and trainers, the music, the magazines and the satellite subscriptions, well know of this association.

I acknowledge my role in this. Aside from articles endorsing the work of rappers, there are several pieces which fill me [with] unease. Like the article solely about Tupac's transgressions, alleged beating of a video director and accused raping of a fan, for a popular monthly music magazine. The commissioning editor, a white university graduate, was visibly gleeful when he asked me to write the piece. Encouraged that a big-budget, international magazine wanted to promote what had previously been an underground music, I enthusiastically went along with it. I regret that now. The highly salacious piece appeared under the headline: "It's Slammer Time! Shot! Jailed! Album Out! . . . Latest."

The editor was excited by the perilous adventures of "gangsta rap" and, in this respect, he was similar to others in significant roles within the hip-hop industry. Whether that was me, as a writer, Jerry Heller, the "money" behind NWA, or national DJs like Radio 1's Tim Westwood.

This voyeuristic tendency wasn't restricted to white people. I had a spot on Kiss FM's weekly rap show and the hosts, DJs Max & Dave, two black men, delighted in the exploits that I relayed. The more outrageous (read: dangerous) the better. We were all, misguidedly, passionate in our justification of the music. So when Bel Mooney condemned gangsta rap and called for a Radio 1 ban in the *Daily Mail* I was outraged and responded with a heartfelt appeal to her that "this would be further suppression of what is already the outpourings of the oppressed."

I wrote that instead of condemning gangsta rap we should instead question the environments that inspired this music.

Celebrating Violence

My views on the dangers of hip-hop began to change in 1997 when the great rapper Notorious BIG, who had overcome a desperate childhood to become a platinum-selling artist, was shot dead in California. I winced again more recently when teenage London rap fan Alex Mulamba was knifed to death in the street, prompting Cameron's comments.

Remorsefully, I accept the role I have played in championing gangsta rap and its attendant lifestyle—but I am not alone. There are DJs, concert promoters, video producers, record company personnel, managers and marketing executives, music outlets and all media who benefit from their association with this lucrative but dangerous genre.

Like basketball and other sports, hip-hop has served as a legitimate route out of the black American ghetto. It has acted as a global conduit that has united people and inspired many other music genres to borrow its beat.

Hip-hop remains hugely relevant, musically and politically; and I still love it. But there is a saturation of one type of rap music that celebrates violence. It's down to economics and the sponsorship deals that many gangsta rappers enjoy, such as 50 Cent's lucrative deal with Reebok, highlight the way many young people are attracted to danger, just as I once was.

As a mother, I fear for them and yearn for the return to prominence of positive rap, such as that made by De La Soul, A Tribe Called Quest and Kanye West. But today, rap's many young impressionable followers are bombarded by the words and imagery of the "Thug Life"—the two words which Tupac had prophetically tattooed across his abdomen before he was shot dead.

> *"If preventing gun violence on campus means restricting black events, then to me, the suggestion seems to be that blackness is the cause of the gun violence."*

Black Music and Black People Do Not Beget Violence

Autumn Carter

In the following viewpoint, Stanford alumna Autumn Carter describes a report of gunshots fired on the Stanford campus. Carter worries that these gunshots will be linked to Blackfest, an R&B and hip-hop festival that drew a largely black crowd. Carter argues that violence cannot be tied to race and says that black events should not be banned from campus. She concludes by hoping for a more open dialogue around race at Stanford. Carter is a political fundraiser who was the editor-in-chief of the Stanford Review, *the student newspaper at Stanford University.*

As you read, consider the following questions:

1. What does Carter say her reaction was to the news of gunfire on campus?
2. According to Carter, what is the problem with suggesting

that race and violence are causally linked?

3. What does Carter say about shooters, attackers, and thieves across the country?

This is the final issue of *The Review* this year. The outgoing Editor-in-Chief usually uses this space to reflect on the past volume of *The Review*.

Until recently, I was prepared to do the same. But instead, I will be using this final editor's note to address a recent campus event that has left me feeling personally unsettled.

Music and Gun Shots

This past weekend, on May 14, [2011] members of the Stanford community received a text message from Stanford police informing them that gun shots were reported from Lagunita parking lot. I'm sure that my reaction was similar to most. I was shocked and a bit rattled.

Stanford is generally considered a "safe" campus. Several highly publicized incidents and attacks this year have highlighted that the campus is not immune to violence, but overall, true concern among students has seemed low.

And yes, though I have been concerned about campus safety since first arriving on this very open campus almost four years ago, I was still shocked by news of gunfire. But I was rattled for a different reason. I was rattled because I anticipated what would come next once news of the shots spread and people began talking.

A musical event called Blackfest was held at Roble Field on May 14. Blackfest features R&B and hip-hop artists, dance performances, and other performances, and the event is open to the public. It drew thousands of individuals from off campus. It drew a largely black crowd.

Honestly, Roble Field is right across the street from where the shots were fired, there were thousands of strangers on campus,

Hip Hop Is Viewed as Violent Because African Americans Are Viewed as Violent

Hip hop gets extra attention for its violent content, and the *perception* of violence is heightened when it appears in rap music form rather than in some other popular genre of music featuring violent imagery. Rappers such as Lil' Jon, Ludacris, 50 Cent, and T.I. who claim that there is violence throughout popular culture and that they get singled out are right: Some violent imagery and lyrics in popular culture are responded to or perceived differently from others. Social psychologist Carrie B. Fried studied this issue and concluded that the perception of violence in rap music lyrics is affected by larger social perception and stereotypes of African-Americans. In her study, she asked participants to respond to lyrics from a folk song about killing a police officer. To some of the participants the song was presented as rap; and to others, as country. Her study supports the hypothesis that lyrics presented as rap music are judged more harshly than the same lyrics presented as country music. She concluded that these identical lyrics seem more violent when featured in rap, perhaps because of the association of rap with the stereotypes of African-Americans.

Tricia Rose, The Hip-Hop Wars: What We Talk About When We Talk About Hip Hop—And Why It Matters. *New York: Basic Books, 2008, pp. 36–37.*

and the shooting was highly unusual for campus. It seems reasonable to assume that the perpetrator was from off-campus and had likely attended Blackfest. And therefore, it was highly probable that he (or she) was black.

But regardless of whether the shooter was on campus for Blackfest or not, I anticipated and feared that the shooting would be linked to race in the absolute wrong way—in a way that suggested a causal relationship between the shooting and race. What I feared was that I would hear snippets like this: *Well, what did you expect? Shooting is what happens when you allow blacks on campus. They will never get to have another black event here.*

I am black. I have been firm and consistent in my assertions that my race is a part of who I am, but that it does not define my individual identity. I have asserted that I am an individual who, like *all* individuals, should be judged by my personal character and merit. This is my conception of identity and race, but I know that not everyone holds it and I know that not everyone at Stanford holds it. This was why I was rattled by the news.

Do Not Ban Black Events

The problem with suggesting that race and violence are causally linked is that it rejects the notion that individuals are rational beings each with their own volition. It suggests that an individual chooses to engage in violence *because* he is black, not that he *chooses* to do so of his own free will. The suggestion that race makes one predisposed to violence cuts the individual, his character, and his will out of the picture. The suggestion that his will has been co-opted by his race is wrong.

I trust that no one actually wants to suggest that one's will can be co-opted by his race, but I am describing the leap that seems to have taken place in minds across campus. Moving from *it is likely that the shooter was black* to *in order to prevent this from happening again, we need to ban black events* is making the jump from correlation to causation when it comes to violence and race.

To prevent something, we must know the cause. If preventing gun violence on campus means restricting black events, then to me, the suggestion seems to be that blackness is the cause of the gun violence.

But judging by crime across the country, we can say that it occurs across all races. Shooters, attackers, and thieves come in all colors and perpetrate acts for different reasons. Indeed, campus shooters, attackers, and thieves come in all colors. Education, age, income, and race may be predictors of violence levels and types, but they are not *causes* of said violence.

Individuals engage in violence. Races do not.

So as I prepare to leave The Farm [Stanford], I want to close with a request: I want to see the dialogue about race broadened and elevated.

Over the last four years, I have witnessed discussions of [race] restricted to and . . . owned by certain groups. Some feel that they are not entitled to engage in the conversations by virtue of their own race, and the result has been a campus that alternates between tiptoeing around and stumbling through race. When they occur, I enjoy seeing and partaking in the frank discussions that are unhampered by feelings of entitlement on any side. There are many issues at Stanford that could benefit from an atmosphere like that, and I truly hope that one day this campus will have it.

Periodical and Internet Sources Bibliography

The following articles have been selected to supplement the diverse views presented in this chapter.

Mihaela Lica Butler	"Sex and Violence in Advertising," *Everything PR*, November 7, 2009. www.pamil-visions.net.
Adam Cohen	"A Supreme Double Standard: If Violent Video Games Are Free Speech, Why Aren't Sexual Images?," *Time*, June 28, 2011. www.time.com.
Samhita Mukhopadhyay	"Sex Is Inappropriate for Minors, But Violence is A-Ok," *Feministing*, June 30, 2011. http://feministing .com.
Carol Potera	"Sex and Violence in the Media Influence Teen Behavior," *American Journal of Nursing*, vol. 109, no. 2, February 2009, p. 20.
Jason Schreier	"Playing the Rape Card: 'Media Psychiatrist' Ratchets up Anti-Videogame Rhetoric," *Ars Technica*, February 2011, http://arstechnica .com.
Roger Simon	"Supreme Court Says Violence Ok. Sex? Maybe," *Politico.com*, June 28, 2011. www.politico.com.
Brandon Soderberg	"The Debate About Rap, Misogyny, and Homophobia," *Spin*, April 22, 2011. www.spin.com.
Stephen Totilo	"The Doctor Who Said Video Games Cause Rape Explains What She Meant," *Kotaku*, February 11, 2011. www.kotaku.com.au.
Marcus Yam	"Poll: Parents More Appalled by Sex Than Severed Heads," *DailyTech*, April 11, 2008. www .dailytech.com.

For Further Discussion

Chapter 1

1. Gordon Dahl and Stefano DellaVigna say that violent movies decrease violent crime. Research cited in the NewsRx article argues that media violence causes aggression. Explain why these two viewpoints do *not* contradict each other.

2. Maura Moynihan argues that Hollywood made torture acceptable to politicians and the public; Scott Horton argues that politicians, by arguing for torture, made it more acceptable for Hollywood and the public. Which do you think is more important, media influence on politics, or the influence of politics on the media?

Chapter 2

1. Based on the viewpoints by the Federal Communications Commission, Adam Thierer, Steven F. Gruel, and James Lileks, do you think that violent media influences children? If it does, does it follow that violence in the media should be regulated by the government? Explain your answer.

2. Has the rating of a movie ever prevented you or someone you know from seeing a film? Based on your answer, and on the viewpoints by the MPAA and FTC, would you say movie ratings are effective or not?

Chapter 3

1. Based on the viewpoints by Barbara J. Wilson and Dan Kennedy, do you believe the news media show too much violence or too little? Are there situations in which the news should make us afraid and anxious, and if so, what are those situations?

2 Do you think Kennedy's argument for uncensored war coverage suggests that the Osama bin Laden death photo should

have been released, as Jimmie L. Foster argues? In explaining the answer, also consider the viewpoint by Hutchinson.

Chapter 4

1. Based on the viewpoint by Robert Scheer, why does the US government restrict depictions of sexuality more severely than depictions of violence? Referring to the *USA Today (Magazine)* viewpoint, do you agree or disagree with the disparity Scheer describes?
2. Can Steve Chapman's article about pornography and sexual violence be used to defend the Kanye West video that Marina DelVecchio discusses? Explain your answer.

Organizations to Contact

The editors have compiled the following list of organizations concerned with the issues debated in this book. The descriptions are derived from materials provided by the organizations. All have publications or information available for interested readers. The list was compiled on the date of publication of the present volume; names, addresses, phone and fax numbers, and e-mail and Internet addresses may change. Be aware that many organizations take several weeks or longer to respond to inquiries, so allow as much time as possible.

American Civil Liberties Union
125 Broad Street
New York, NY 10004
(212) 549-2627
website: www.aclu.org

Founded in 1920, the American Civil Liberties Union is dedicated to defending the constitutional rights of all Americans in court and in legislatures. The organization is opposed to the censoring of any form of speech, including media violence. Handbooks, project and public policy reports, and other publications are available on the organization's website.

American Psychological Association (APA)
750 First Street NE
Washington, DC
(800) 374-2721
e-mail: publicaffairs@apa.org
website: www.apa.org

The APA is a professional society of psychologists that seeks to promote the field of psychology as a science and profession. The association has conducted numerous studies causally linking exposure to media violence with violent behavior and aggression. The APA advocates for a reduction of violent content in video games and other media and supports content-based ratings warning consumers of the level of portrayed violence. Its website includes numerous reports, press releases, and journal articles concerning the impact of media violence.

Australia Council on Children and the Media (ACCM)
PO Box 447
Glenelg SA 5045
Australia
+61 8 8376-2111 • fax: +61 8 8376-2122
e-mail: info@youngmedia.org.au
website: www.youngmedia.org.au

ACCM is a not-for-profit company that provides educational resources and engages in advocacy to encourage families, industry, and decision makers in building and maintaining a media environment that fosters the health, safety, and well-being of Australian children. Its publications include *small screen*, a monthly news review; *Mind Over Media* fact sheets available in PDF form; and books and articles available through its website. The site also includes an extensive list of movie reviews.

Canadians Concerned About Violence in Entertainment (C-CAVE)
167 Glen Road
Toronto ON M4W 2W8
Canada
e-mail: info@c-cave.com
website: www.c-cave.com

C-CAVE aims to educate the public about the impact of media violence on society. The organization provides general information to the public through its website as well as by participating in public forums and lectures. C-CAVE views increased media literacy, in combination with sensible government regulations and self-regulation for the entertainment industry, as the cornerstones of achieving a safer society. The C-CAVE website offers numerous articles and links to other organizations combating violent entertainment.

Cato Institute

1000 Massachusetts Avenue NW
Washington, DC 20001-5403
(202) 842-0200 • fax: (202) 842-3490
website: www.cato.org

The Cato Institute is a libertarian public policy research foundation dedicated to increasing the understanding of public policies based on the principles of limited government, free markets, individual liberty, and peace. As such, it opposes government regulation of the media and of media violence. It publishes the triannual *Cato Journal*; the periodic *Cato Policy Analysis*; and a bimonthly newsletter, *Cato Policy Review*.

Center for Media Literacy (CML)

23852 Pacific Coast Highway #472
Malibu, CA 90265
(310) 456-1225 • fax: (310) 456-0020
e-mail: cml@medialit.org
website: www.medialit.org

CML seeks to increase critical analysis of the media through its publication of educational materials and Medialit Kits. CML was founded on the belief that media literacy is an essential skill in the twenty-first century as varying media forms become evermore omnipresent in everyday life, and individuals should be empowered from a young age to make informed choices about the media they consume. *CONNECTIONS* is the official newsletter of the organization, with archival issues available online. Additional informative materials are available by topic on the CML website.

Entertainment Software Ratings Board (ESRB)

317 Madison Avenue, 22nd Floor
New York, NY 10017
website: www.esrb.org

ESRB was founded in 1994 to be the self-regulating body for the entertainment gaming industry. The board has been charged with multiple duties including: determining content-based ratings for computer and video games, enforcing advertising guidelines set by the industry, and ensuring online privacy practices for Internet gaming. The ESRB was created to aid all consumers, especially families, in making appropriate decisions about which games to purchase. Additional information about the ratings system and current projects by the ESRB can be read on the board's website.

Federal Communications Commission (FCC)

445 12th Street SW
Washington, DC 20554
(888) 225-5322 • fax: (866) 448-0232
e-mail: fccinfo@fcc.gov
website: www.fcc.gov

The FCC, an independent government agency, regulates telecommunications within the United States. It is responsible for creating and implementing policies for interstate and international communication by radio, television, wire, satellite, and cable. Additionally, the FCC reviews all educational programming created by the networks. Reports, updates, and reviews published by the FCC are accessible on the commission's website.

National Cable and Telecommunications Association (NCTA)

25 Massachusetts Avenue NW, Suite 100
Washington, DC 20001
(202) 222-2300

website: www.ncta.com

The NCTA is the cable industry's major trade association. It provides the cable operators serving the majority of Americans with a single unified voice to address and speak out on issues affecting the industry. The association also works closely with Congress, the courts, and the US public to ensure that public policies dealing with cable television are advanced. Its website includes various reports and news releases.

Parents Television Council (PTC)
707 Wilshire Boulevard #2075
Los Angeles, CA 90017
(213) 403-1300 • fax: (213) 403-4301
e-mail: editor@parentstv.org
website: www.parentstv.org

Established originally as a special project of the Media Research Center, the PTC has continued its primary mission of promoting responsible and decent programming in response to the US public's demand for such shows. The PTC publishes the *Family Guide to Prime Time Television* yearly, assessing every sitcom and drama broadcast on the major networks and providing detailed information about their content. Additional publications, such as current television and movie reviews, are available on the organization's website.

Bibliography of Books

Craig A. Anderson, Douglas A. Gentile, and Katherine E. Buckley

Violent Video Game Effects on Children and Adolescents: Theory, Research and Public Policy. New York: Oxford University Press, 2007.

Emilie Buchwald, Pamela Fletcher, and Martha Roth, eds.

Transforming a Rape Culture, 2nd ed. Minneapolis: Milkweed Editions, 2005.

Francis G. Couvares, ed.

Movie Censorship and American Culture, 2nd ed. Amherst: University of Massachusetts Press, 2006.

Rusel DeMaria

Reset: Changing the Way We Look at Video Games. San Francisco: Berrett-Koehler Publishers, Inc., 2007.

Kate Egan

Trash or Treasure?: Censorship and the Changing Meaning of the Video Nasties. Manchester, UK: Manchester University Press, 2008.

Dave Grossman and Gloria Degaetano

Stop Teaching Our Kids to Kill: A Call to Action Against TV, Movie and Video Game Violence. New York: Crown Publishers, 1999.

Steffen Hantke

The American Horror Film: The Genre at the Turn of the Millennium. Jackson: Mississippi University Press, 2010.

Drew Humphries	*Women, Violence, and the Media: Readings in Feminist Criminology.* Lebanon, NH: Northeastern University Press, 2009.
Gerard Jones	*Killing Monsters: Why Children Need Fantasy, Super-Heroes, and Make-Believe Violence.* New York: Basic Books, 2002.
Jean Kilbourne and Mary Pipher	*Can't Buy My Love: How Advertising Changes the Way We Think and Feel.* New York: Touchstone, 1999.
Steven J. Kirsh	*Children, Adolescents, and Media Violence: A Critical Look at the Research.* Thousand Oaks, CA: Sage Publications, 2006.
Steven J. Kirsh	*Media and Youth: A Developmental Perspective.* Malden, MA: Wiley-Blackwell, 2009.
Eric Lichtenfeld	*Action Speaks Louder: Violence, Spectacle, and the American Action Movie.* Westport, CT: Greenwood Publishing Group, 2007.
Jane McGonigal	*Reality Is Broken: Why Games Make Us Better and How They Can Change The World.* New York: Penguin Press, 2011.

Jeffrey O.G. Ogbar	*Hip-Hop Revolution: The Culture and Politics of Rap.* Lawrence: University Press of Kansas, 2007.
W. James Potter	*The 11 Myths of Media Violence.* Thousand Oaks, CA: Sage Publications, 2003.
Tricia Rose	*The Hip Hop Wars: What We Talk About When We Talk About Hip Hop.* London: Perseus Books Group, 2008.
Aric Sigman	*Remotely Controlled: How Television Is Damaging Our Lives.* New York: Random House, 2005.
Victor C. Strasburger, Barbara J. Wilson, and Amy B. Jordan, eds.	*Children, Adolescents, and the Media.* Thousand Oaks, CA: Sage Publications, 2009.
Gwyn Symonds	*The Aesthetics of Violence in Contemporary Media.* London: Continuum, 2012.
Stephen Vaughn	*Freedom and Entertainment: Rating the Movies in an Age of New Media.* New York: Cambridge University Press, 2006.
S. Craig Watkins	*Hip Hop Matters: Politics, Pop Culture, and the Struggle for the Soul of a Movement.* Boston: Beacon Press, 2005.

Jennifer Hart Weed, Richard Brian Davis, and Ronald Weed	*24 and Philosophy: The World According to Jack*. Malden, MA: Blackwell Publishing, 2008.
Jeremy Wisnewski	*Understanding Torture*. Edinburgh, UK: Edinburgh University Press, 2010.
Rick Worland	*The Horror Film: An Introduction*. Malden, MA: Blackwell Publishing, 2007.

Index